CONTRAC
ADMINISTRA

FOR ARCHITECTS AND QUANTITY SURVEYORS

Fifth Edition
with Supplement on
the JCT 1980 Form

THE AQUA GROUP

GRANADA
London Toronto Sydney New York

Granada Publishing Limited – Technical Books Division
Frogmore, St Albans, Herts AL2 2NF
and
36 Golden Square, London W1R 4AH
866 United Nations Plaza, New York, NY 10017, USA
117 York Street, Sydney, NSW 2000, Australia
100 Skyway Avenue, Rexdale, Ontario, Canada, M9W 3A6
61 Beach Road, Auckland, New Zealand

First published in Great Britain 1965 by Crosby Lockwood & Son Ltd
Second edition 1972
Third edition published by Granada Publishing Limited
in Crosby Lockwood Staples, 1975
Fourth edition published by Granada Publishing Limited, 1979
(original ISBN 0 258 97139 8)
Fifth edition 1981
Reprinted 1982

British Library Cataloguing in Publication Data
Aqua Group
Contract administration for architects and quantity surveyors. – 5th ed.
1. Building – Contracts and specifications – Great Britain.
I. Title.
692'.8'0941   TH425   80-41791

ISBN 0-246-11555-6

Printed in Great Britain by Richard Clay (The Chaucer Press) Ltd, Bungay, Suffolk

Granada ®
Granada Publishing ®

Other titles by the Aqua Group

Pre-Contract Practice for Architects and Quantity Surveyors, Sixth Edition
Which Builder? Tendering and Contractual Arrangements

CONTENTS

PUBLISHER'S NOTE

Fifth Edition

Pages 3–83 of this book deal with contracts placed under the 1963 edition of the JCT Form (July 1977 revision), many of which will continue to run for some years.

The Supplement on pages 84–117 details the main changes under the 1980 JCT Form, now in use.

It is important to note that the main text (pages 3–83) also deals with points of good practice and the Supplement should be read in conjunction with this.

AUTHORS' NOTE

Pre-Contract Practice for Architects and Quantity Surveyors, now in its sixth edition, sets out what we believe to be the best way of performing our respective duties in the pre-contract stages of a building project.

In *Contract Administration* we proceed from the receipt of tenders to the placing of the contract through the whole post-contract period to the settlement of the final account. Again we have endeavoured to put down what we believe is the best way of doing things, but we acknowledge that no two professional firms conduct themselves in an identical manner and our main purpose is to indicate the standard of practice and procedure required for the proper administration of a contract.

Since the publication of the Fourth Edition in 1979, the new JCT (1980) Form of Contract has been published. For many years, however, the 1963 JCT Form of Contract will continue to be used on contracts which were in preparation before the publication of the 1980 Form. Furthermore, it will be some four or five years before extensive experience of the 1980 Form has been established. We therefore are publishing a supplement to the Fourth Edition indicating the main points to be observed on the 1980 Form and this can be used where contracts on the new form are being let.

We are particularly indebted to Peter Johnson, who has prepared the information on the JCT 1980 form so comprehensively and which has formed the basis of the supplement to this edition. Frank Johnstone has revised the index.

We are also once again indebted to the Royal Institute of British Architects, the Royal Insitution of Chartered Surveyors and the Institution of Civil Engineers for their kind permission to reproduce several of their standard forms.

The sketches are by Brian Bagnall.

Tony Brett-Jones CBE, FRICS, FCIArb (Chairman)
Brian Bagnall BArch (L'pool)
Peter Johnson FRICS, FCIArb
Frank Johnstone FRICS
Alfred Lester DipArch, RIBA
John Oakes FRICS, FCIArb
Geoffrey Poole FRIBA, ACIArb
Colin Rice FRICS
John Townsend FRICS
James Williams DA(Edin), FRIBA

Introduction

INTRODUCTION TO FIFTH EDITION

When we asked Sir Basil Spence, then President of the Royal Institute of British Architects, to contribute a foreword to the first edition of *Pre-Contract Practice for Architects and Quantity Surveyors* he wrote, 'The ideal would be for all drawings and bills of quantities to be complete, all consultants, specialists and sub-contractors nominated, and in fact all book and paper work to be ready before the work on the site actually starts so that the builder knows exactly what he is expected to do and can plan accordingly.' *Pre-Contract Practice,* now in its sixth edition, is a practical guide to good pre-contract procedure written with that ideal in mind.

For a variety of reasons it is not always possible even to aim at the ideal which Sir Basil Spence described. Indeed, it was because we recognized the many different ways in which building contracts can be let that we wrote *Which Builder? – Tendering and Contractual Arrangements,* which gives an outline of the various methods which can be adopted and the circumstances in which it is appropriate to use them. Where, however, the traditional method is used, experience has shown that it can be very effective in practice if the ideal described by Sir Basil Spence is fulfilled. This should always be the target and architects and quantity surveyors should base their practice on that ideal. Even when circumstances necessitate procedures being modified, the basic principles of good practice set out in the book will still apply.

In this present book, *Contract Administration,* we endeavour to set out a practical guide to good procedure during the contract period, that is to say from the acceptance of the tender to the issue of the final certificate.

Inevitably in the pre-contract stage everything of consequence must be committed to paper in the form of drawings, schedules, bills of quantities, specification notes, annotations of the bills of quantities, estimates and so on. In the course of this book we shall demonstrate the important part that good paper-work plays in the smooth running of a building contract. We do not advocate committing all sorts of things to paper just to fill up the office files, but we do contend that clear instructions and good records lead to efficient, economical building and to a fair settlement at the end, free from argument and dispute. We also attach considerable importance to etiquette and procedure; again not just for their own sakes, but because good manners lead to harmonious working and respect for the other man's point of view.

This edition of *Contract Administration* is being published at a time when the 1963 edition of the JCT Standard Form of Contract, with its various amendments, is about to be replaced by the 1980 edition. At the time of writing, new contracts are still being entered into on the 1963 edition and many current contracts on that edition still have a long way to go before completion. The main body of the book, therefore, is still based on the 1963 conditions and has been written against the background of our collective experience of working to those conditions during the past 17 years.

1

Like the majority of our professional colleagues we have as yet no experience of the 1980 Standard Form of Building Contract in practice, but we have considered its likely impact on our work and we have added a Supplement to this book in which we draw attention to those changes in the Standard Form which will affect the day-to-day administration of building contracts. This Supplement must be read against the background of the main body of the book. It is not intended as a legal treatise on the new Conditions, nor does it attempt to discuss the pros and cons of the changes which have been made. We see it more as a guide to the matters to which we as practising architects and quantity surveyors must give attention and fresh thought in our work.

The 1980 Standard Form can be expected to come into general use during 1981. It looks very different from earlier editions and it does contain a number of significant changes and these are dealt with in the Supplement. However, the principles of good practice which we have described in *Contract Administration* still apply and those practitioners who have adopted those principles in the past will find that the new procedures and rules embodied in the 1980 Standard Form are not nearly as unfamiliar as they may at first appear to be.

Before proceeding further we must stress that in this book, as in the case of *Pre-Contract Practice,* our observations are intended to apply to a typical and reasonably normal building project in which the JCT Standard Form of Building Contract, with quantities, is used. In the main body of the book we have assumed that the 1963 edition (July 1977 revision) applies and it is this document to which we refer when writing about 'The Conditions of Contract'. In the Supplement dealing with the new Contract we use the short description '1980 Standard Form'. Although detailed procedures will vary according to the form of contract used, the general approach which we advocate throughout the book can be applied to most types of building contract. We refer throughout the book to 'the architect' but it will be appreciated that when the Local Authorities edition of the Contract is in use such references would equally apply to the Supervising Officer.

We would like to stress that to avoid confusion and, in particular, unintended consequences, Standard Forms of Contract should be used as printed. Alterations are rarely necessary and almost always dangerous.

In the final chapter of *Pre-Contract Practice* we dealt with tendering procedure and it is from that point that we advance into the period of contract work itself. In accordance with good practice it has been assumed that tenders have been obtained on the principles set out in *The Code of Procedure for Single Stage Selective Tendering* published by the Joint Consultative Committee of Architects, Quantity Surveyors and Builders. In the course of this process of obtaining tenders the contractors will have been provided with the most comprehensive information about the work and the form of contract that it is practicable to send out and, most important, they should have been allowed adequate time for preparing their tenders.

If the achievement of a high standard of pre-contract work is followed by a businesslike approach to the tendering, the actual construction of the building will have got away to the best possible start.

October 1980

Chapter 1
THE BUILDING TEAM

In this book we are using the term 'building team' in its widest sense, that is:

employer
architect
quantity surveyor
structural consultant
services consultants

together comprising the 'design team', plus the

contractor
foreman
nominated sub-contractors
nominated suppliers
clerk of works.

Of its members the employer, the architect, the quantity surveyor, the contractor, the nominated sub-contractors and suppliers and the clerk of works are mentioned in the JCT Form of Contract. The consulting engineers are not, and their position will depend largely on what form of agreement they have with the employer or the architect. Where they have supervisory duties they should be named in the bills of quantities, but they have no power under the contract and if they wish to issue instructions this must be done through the architect.

The clerk of works is normally appointed by the employer to act, under the direction of the architect, solely as an inspector of the works. He is likely to be an experienced tradesman e.g. carpenter and joiner or bricklayer, and will usually be recommended by the architect. He should be ready to take up his duties about two weeks before the possession date and will be resident on site for the duration of the contract. On larger buildings, particularly those with a high services element, he will be assisted by specialist clerks of works whose appointments will be for varying periods; in some instances resident engineers will fulfil these functions.

It is as well to remember that the building contract is between the employer and the contractor, and although the architect and the quantity surveyor figure in it, and many clauses include the words 'the Architect shall . . .', these two professional advisors are not parties to the agreement. Therefore if the architect or quantity surveyor fails to carry out any of his duties as defined in the agreement and the contractor considers he has a grievance, his only contractual redress is with the employer.

The 1963 edition of the JCT Form of Contract is exhaustive on the subject of the rights, duties and liabilities of various members of the building team, and each member of the team should be familiar with the contract as a whole, and particularly

3

with those clauses directly concerning his own work. In this book, references to the Form of Contract are to the July 1977 revision.

It is not our intention that this volume should be a handbook on the current form of contract but some of the more important points as they concern individual members of the building team are listed below with the relevant clauses given:

The employer

P. 1	Name and address;
P. 1	Appointment of architect;
Cl. 2	Power to employ others if contractor does not comply with instructions;
Cl. 3	Duties in relation to confidential nature of contract documents;
Cl. 10	Power to appoint clerk of works;
Cl. 16	Procedure as to partial possession by the employer;
Cl. 17	Rights as to assignment of contract;
Cl. 19, 20	Powers, duties and liabilities as to insurance;
Cl. 21	Duty to give contractor possession of site;
Cl. 22	Powers to deduct damages in respect of non-completion;
Cl. 25	Power to determine contract and procedure;
Cl. 25	Rights and duties in event of contractor's bankruptcy;
Cl. 26	Duties in respect of determination of contract through own bankruptcy;
Cl. 27	No liability to nominated sub-contractors;
Cl. 29	Power to engage artists and tradesmen, and responsibility;
Cl. 30	Powers and duties concerning certificates;
Cl. 32	Rights and obligations in event of war;
Cl. 33	Rights as to war damage;
Cl. 34	Rights regarding 'finds';
Cl. 35	Rights, liabilities and procedure in respect of arbitration; VAT supplemental agreement.

The contractor

P. 1	Name and address;
Cl. 1	General obligations;
Cl. 1	Duties as to discrepancies;
Cl. 2	Compliance with architect's instructions;
Cl. 2	Right to challenge architect's instructions and power to confirm instructions;
Cl. 3	Duty to keep documents on site;
Cl. 3	Duty to return drawings to architect if asked;
Cl. 3	Duties as to confidential nature of contract documents;
Cl. 4	Duties as to statutory consents and to indemnify employer against statutory charges;
Cl. 5	Duties in setting-out;
Cl. 6	Duty to comply with standards;
Cl. 6	Liability to bear direct and consequential costs resulting from faulty workmanship;
Cl. 7	Duty to indemnify employer against royalty and patent claims;
Cl. 8	Duty to keep foreman permanently on job;

Cl. 9	Duty to provide access for architect to job and workshop;
Cl. 11	Rights as to variations;
Cl. 14	Ownership and responsibility for unfixed materials;
Cl. 15	Duties and rights as to making good defects;
Cl. 16	Duties and procedure as to partial possession by the employer;
Cl. 17	Limitations as to sub-letting and assignment;
Cl. 18	Liabilities in respect of personal injury and of damage;
Cl. 19	Duties regarding general insurance;
Cl. 20	Duties regarding fire insurance;
Cl. 21	Duty to proceed diligently with the works;
Cl. 22	Liabilities in event of non-completion;
Cl. 23	Duty to inform architect of delays and rights regarding delays;
Cl. 24	Procedure for seeking reimbursement in event of disturbance of the works;
Cl. 25	Rights and duties in respect of determination of contract by employer;
Cl. 25	Duties in respect of determination of contract through own bankruptcy;
Cl. 26	Power to determine contract and procedure;
Cl. 26	Power to determine contract in event of employer's bankruptcy and procedure;
Cl. 27	Implied duty to bind nominated sub-contractors;
Cl. 27	Right to object to nominated sub-contractors;
Cl. 28	Implied duty to bind suppliers;
Cl. 29	Duty to allow other artists and tradesmen on to site;
Cl. 30	Procedure regarding certificates and duties to nominated sub-contractors;
Cl. 31	Procedure on fluctuations;
Cl. 32	Rights and obligations in event of war;
Cl. 33	Duties as to war damage;
Cl. 34	Duties regarding 'finds' and rights as to reimbursement;
Cl. 35	Rights, liabilities and procedure in respect of arbitration;
	VAT supplemental agreement.

The architect

P. 1 & 2	Name and address;
Cl. 2	Duty to justify instructions;
Cl. 2	Duty to issue instructions in writing;
Cl. 3	Custody of contract documents;
Cl. 3	Duties concerning furnishing copies of drawings and documents;
Cl. 3	Power to require return of drawings on completion;
Cl. 3	Duties in relation to confidential nature of contract documents;
Cl. 5	Duties as to setting-out;
Cl. 6	Powers as to opening up of suspect work;
Cl. 6	Powers as to removal of faulty work;
Cl. 6	Power to instruct dismissal of persons from job;
Cl. 9	Right of access to job and workshops;
Cl. 11	Powers and duties regarding variations, prime cost sums and provisional sums;
Cl. 12	Duty as to errors in bills of quantities;
Cl. 14	Powers regarding removal of unfixed goods;
Cl. 15	Duty to issue certificate of practical completion;
Cl. 15	Duty as to schedule of defects;

'Sectional Completion Supplement'.

This supplement can be incorporated in the contract to adapt it for use where the works are to be completed by phased sections.

Many of the clauses quoted above will have to be invoked only if the contract is not running smoothly and the primary duty of the building team is to see that it does. It is generally agreed that the origin of contractual disputes is seldom found in actual dishonesty or plain incompetence of any party, but rather in the failure of the architect, contractor, or whoever it may be to put his intentions or thoughts across successfully – in other words a failure of communications.

'Communications' have of late years been the subject of books, conferences and papers and it is a matter with which we cannot hope to deal exhaustively here. Nevertheless we set out below certain golden rules to be observed by all members of the building team in their dealings with each other:

1. Do not tamper with the standard clauses of the building contract.
2. Ensure that the contract documents remain in the custody of the architect or the quantity surveyor and that all users have certified copies.
3. Use realistic figures in the appendix to the building contract.
4. Where alterations exist or where entries have to be made in the appendix, this information must also be in the bills of quantities at tender stage.
5. All instructions to the contractor must be channelled through the architect.
6. All instructions to sub-contractors or suppliers must be channelled through the contractor.
7. For routine matters such as instructions, site reports, minutes of meetings, and valuations for certificates, use standardised forms rather than letters.
8. Circulate to those who need to be kept informed as well as to those who need to act.
9. Be precise and unambiguous.
10. Act promptly.

Examples of suggested standardised layouts for the more important communications passing between members of the building team are given in later chapters.

The building team

7

Chapter 2

PLACING THE CONTRACT

The placing of the contract is a relatively simple routine matter but the events which immediately precede it and those which follow immediately afterwards are of great importance.

The receipt of tenders and their examination were dealt with in *Pre-Contract Practice*. It may be assumed, therefore, that the quantity surveyor, after examining the bills of quantities of the lowest tenderer, will have reported to the architect, who will in turn have submitted a report to the employer. The employer should be encouraged to make an early decision on that report for it is of the utmost importance to a contractor to know quickly whether or not his tender has been successful.

If no serious errors have been found in the bills of the lowest tenderer the architect's report will normally recommend acceptance of that tender. Where the widely accepted practice of selective tendering has been followed, acceptance of other than the lowest tender should be considered only in most exceptional circumstances. An invitation to the contractor to tender for a job should not be issued if it is not intended to place the contract with him if he is lowest and best value for money.

Probably the employer will accept the architect's recommendation and as soon as he does so all contractors who tendered should be notified and sent a list of the tenders received. If priced bills of quantities have been submitted at the same time as the tenders, these should be returned to the unsuccessful contractors unopened.

Errors in bills of quantities

In the course of his examination of the priced bills of quantities the quantity surveyor may have found some errors in pricing or arithmetic, or perhaps in both. If these were of a very minor nature they may be ignored. If, however, they were more serious the contractor should have been advised of them before the report is submitted to the employer.

The invitation to tender will have stated which of the alternatives under section 6 of the NJCC Code of Procedure for Single-stage Selective Tendering 1977 was to apply. Under alternative 1 the contractor will have been given the opportunity of withdrawing if he is not prepared to stand by his tender and under alternative 2 he will have been given the opportunity of correcting genuine errors.

Whichever circumstances apply, errors must be dealt with in the appropriate way in order to put the bills of quantities right for their use as a contract document.

If alternative 1 applies and the contractor has agreed to stand by his tender the errors should be put right, the arithmetic corrected and the summary amended as necessary. An adjustment should then be made at the end of the summary which will leave the final total of the bills equalling the original tender figure. This adjustment will be a lump sum equal to the net amount of the errors and will be added to or deducted from the corrected total of the summary. A note should be added in which the amount of the adjustment is expressed as a percentage of the total value of the general contractor's work (i.e. the total of the bills less preliminary items, contingencies and prime cost and provision sums). Any rates in the bills subsequently used for valuing variations or interim certificates will then be adjusted by this percentage.

If alternative 2 applies, the errors will be corrected in the same way and the summary amended, but no adjustment will be made to restore the total to the original tender figure, the revised summary total becoming the contract sum.

Signing the contract

While the contract documents are being prepared the architect should settle with the contractor the dates for possession of the site and completion of the work, if these have not already been decided. He should make arrangements with the contractor for the initial site meeting and at this stage he should also ensure that the contractor has no valid objection to any nominated sub-contractor or supplier.

Once these matters have been settled the contract documents should be signed. These normally consist of the Articles of Agreement, drawings showing the extent and nature of the works and the bills of quantities.

It must be borne in mind that in addition to completing the Articles of Agreement at the front of the JCT Form of Contract, it is also necessary to make a number of deletions in the text of the Conditions. These deletions are as follows:

Clause 12(1) – applicable edition of the Standard Method of Measurement.
Clause 20 – responsibility for insurance against fire and other risks.
Clause 23(j) – optional sub-clauses regarding extension of time.
Clause 30B(2)(a) – Employer's status in respect of the Statutory Tax Deduction Scheme.
Clause 31 – alternative clauses regarding fluctuations.

It may also be necessary to amend clause 35 regarding arbitration if English law and/or the provisions of the Arbitration Act 1950 are not to apply.

These deletions and amendments will have have been notified to the contractors in the bills of quantities at the time of tendering and no other deletions or amendments should be made without the prior agreement of the contractor. All deletions and amendments must be initialled by the parties at the time the contract documents are signed.

It is also necessary to complete the appendix to the Conditions of Contract and here again the information to be inserted will have been stated in the bills of quantities. In the event of any item in the appendix having been left for decision until after tenders have been submitted, the matter must be agreed with the contractor before the contract documents are completed.

There are two supplements to the JCT Form of Contract which must also be dealt with at this stage. The first of these is the Supplemental Agreement dealing with Value Added Tax. This is bound in with the JCT Form and must be completed and signed in all cases. The second supplement is that dealing with sectional completion of the works and is optional.

It is important to distinguish between the Sectional Completion Supplement and clause 16 of the JCT 'Partial Possession by Employer'. The Sectional Completion Supplement enables the JCT Form of Contract to be adapted so as to be suitable for use where the works are to be completed by phased sections. It can only be used

CONTRACT ADMINISTRATION

where tenderers are notified that the employer requires the works to be carried out by phased sections of which the employer will take possession on the practical completion of each section. If the work has not been divided into sections in the tender documents the supplement cannot be used. In such cases, if the employer wishes to take possession of parts of the work during the course of the contract, the provisions of clause 16 will apply but it must be noted that under that clause the prior consent of the contractor must be obtained.

If provision has been made for including the Sectional Completion Supplement in the contract documents, the first page of the Articles of Agreement in the Form must be amended or replaced by the equivalent page in the supplement and the appendix in the JCT Form must be deleted and replaced by the appendix in the supplement.

Many authorities and public companies prefer to execute their contracts under seal, although since 1960 such bodies have been able to enter into contract by the signature of an authorised official. As far as building contracts are concerned, the only material difference between a contract under hand and a contract under seal is that in the case of the latter the contractor's liability for latent defects is extended from six years to twelve years by virtue of section 2 of the Limitation Act 1939. Even this distinction, however, may now have been undermined by the decision of the House of Lords in the case of *Anns and others* v. *The London Borough of Merton*. Whether or not a contract is to be under seal is a matter entirely for the parties and they should be consulted on this point before the contract documents are prepared. There is, incidentally, no objection to a contract being signed by one party and sealed by the other.

In August 1970, under the finance act of that year, stamping of contracts under hand was abolished. If the contract is under seal, however, a 50p stamp must be impressed within thirty days of execution.

Clause 3 of the conditions of contract requires that the contract documents be held by the architect or quantity surveyor so as to be available at all reasonable times for inspection by the employer or the contractor.

The employer may require the contractor to provide a bond for the due performance of the contract. Such a bond will normally be obtained by the contractor from an insurance company or a bank, or alternatively, where the contractor is a subsidiary company of a larger organisation, it may take the form of a guarantee from the parent company. The bond holder or guarantor and the terms of the bond must, of course, be approved by the employer and the amount or surety provided will normally be 10% of the contract sum, this amount becoming available to the employer to meet any additional expense he incurs as a result of the contractor failing to execute the contract or otherwise being in breach of his obligations under it.

Whether or not a bond is required is one of those matters which must be settled before the documents are sent out to tender so that the contractor, who is responsible for all costs in connection with the bond, can include those costs in his price.

There is no standard form of bond published specifically for building works, but most bonds are similar in form and we reproduce in example 1 the standard form incorporated in the Institution of Civil Engineers (ICE) Conditions of Contract. An example of a bond in the form of a parent company guarantee is shown in example 2.

Issue of documents

Also in accordance with clause 3, immediately after the signing of the contract the architect must furnish the contractor with:

10

(i) One copy certified on behalf of the employer of the Articles of Agreement and Conditions.
(ii) Two copies of the contract drawings.
(iii) Two copies of the unpriced bills of quantities, and (if requested by the contractor) one copy of the contract bills.

If the bills of quantities referred to above have not been annotated, the architect must also provide the contractor with two copies of the specification or equivalent document. This document must not vary in any way from the contract documents i.e. articles of agreement, conditions of contract, drawings and bills.

Insurances

Before the work commences the architect must satisfy himself that all insurances required by the contract have been taken out. These consist of the insurances called for under clauses 19 and 20.

Clause 19(1) deals with insurance against injury to persons and property and is the responsibility of the contractor. It is usually covered by his own comprehensive policy and the architect should verify that this is the case. He should ensure that the cover provided is not less than that stated in the Appendix to the Conditions of Contract, and he should ascertain that the current premiums have been paid. Clause 19(2), which was the source of a great deal of difficulty until revised in 1968, deals with insurance against specific risks which are listed in the clause together with risks which are excepted. If in the pre-contract period it has been decided that insurance is required under this clause, a provisional sum to cover the premium will have been included in the bills of quantities. Before the work commences, therefore, the architect should issue instructions to the contractor regarding the expenditure of this provisional sum. Although required to be in the joint names of the employer and the contractor, this insurance is the contractor's responsibility and, depending on circumstances, it may be advisable to arrange a meeting with the contractor's insurance company to ensure that the risks are clearly understood and that the cover is adequate. After instructions have been issued, the architect should verify that the necessary policy has been taken out, or that the contractor's public liability policy has been suitably extended or endorsed, and that the premium has been paid.

Clause 20 deals with the insurance of the works against fire and other risks and may be the responsibility of either the employer or the contractor according to the circumstances of the job. It is therefore particularly important to ensure that the party concerned has obtained the necessary cover and paid the premium, and that the two parties are not each leaving the matter to the other.

When building work is to be carried out to existing premises which are in everyday use, the employer should be advised to consult his insurance broker and explain what is being proposed so that any necessary adjustments can be made to his normal insurances.

It must be borne in mind that when a new building is being erected adjacent to existing buildings, or where existing buildings are being altered, there may well be additional risks to the existing building or to the employer's stock or machinery arising from the very presence of the work, but not covered by clause 20 of the Conditions of Contract. Similarly, during the course of a contract, the employer may wish to install equipment or machinery in a new building with his own work force or under a separate contract. In such circumstances the employer and contractor should establish the responsibility of insurance of these items. It is essential, therefore, that the whole matter of insurance is discussed with the employer before the contract commences so that all risks are adequately covered.

Analysis of tender

Finally, during the process of the placing of the contract the quantity surveyor will carry out any analysis of the tender that the employer or the architect may require, at the same time bringing his cost plan up-to-date thus establishing a proper basis for cost control during the execution of the work.

"not prepared to stand by his tender"

EXAMPLE 1

Form of Bond

BY THIS BOND ¹We ....

of .... in the

County of .... ²We .... Limited

whose registered office is at .... in the

County of .... ; ³We ....

and .... carrying on business in partnership under

the name or style of ....

at .... in the

County of .... (hereinafter called " the Contractor ") ⁴and ....

.... of ....

in the County of .... and

of .... in the County of ....

.... ⁵and .... Limited

whose registered office is at .... in the

County of .... (hereinafter called " the ⁴Sureties/Surety ") are held and firmly

bound unto .... (hereinafter

called " the Employer ") in the sum of .... pounds

(£ ....) for the payment of which sum the Contractor and the ⁴Sureties/Surety bind

themselves their successors and assigns jointly and severally by these presents.

Sealed with our respective seals and dated this .... day of ....

19 ....

WHEREAS the Contractor by an Agreement made between the Employer of the one part and the Contractor of the other part has entered into a Contract (hereinafter called "the said Contract ") for the construction and completion of the Works and maintenance of the Permanent Works as therein mentioned in conformity with the provisions of the said Contract.

NOW THE CONDITION of the above-written Bond is such that if the Contractor shall duly perform and observe all the terms provisions conditions and stipulations of the said Contract on the Contractor's part to be performed and observed according to the true purport intent and meaning thereof or if on default by the Contractor the Sureties/Surety shall satisfy and discharge the damages sustained by the Employer thereby up to the amount of the above-written Bond then this obligation shall be null and void but otherwise shall be and remain in full force and effect but no alteration in terms of the said Contract made by agreement between the Employer and the Contractor or in the extent or nature of the Works to be constructed completed and maintained thereunder and no allowance of time by the Employer or the Engineer under the said Contract nor any forbearance or forgiveness in or in respect of any matter or thing concerning the said Contract on the part of the Employer or the said Engineer shall in any way release the Sureties/Surety from any liability under the above-written Bond.

Signed Sealed and Delivered by the said }
   in the presence of:—

The Common Seal of
                    LIMITED }
was hereunto affixed in the presence of:— }

(Similar forms of Attestation Clause for the Sureties or Surety)

---

1 Is appropriate to an individual, **2** to a Limited Company and **3** to a Firm. Strike out whichever two are inappropriate.

4 Is appropriate where there are two individual Sureties, **5** where the Surety is a Bank or Insurance Company. Strike out whichever is inappropriate.

14

EXAMPLE 2

THIS DEED is made the . . . . day

of . . . . 197 . . . . BETWEEN . . . . whose

registered office is at . . . . (hereinafter

called "the Guarantor") of the one part and . . . .

. . . . whose registered office is at

. . . .

(hereinafter called "the Employer") of the other part

WHEREAS

(1) This Agreement is supplemental to a contract (hereinafter

called "the Contract") dated the . . . . day of . . . . 197 . . . .

and made between the Employer of the one part and . . . .

whose registered office is at . . . .

(hereinafter called "the Contractors") of the other part whereby the Contractors agreed and undertook to

carry out the following works . . . .

. . . .

. . . .

(2) The Guarantor has agreed the due performance of the contract in manner hereinafter appearing

NOW THIS DEED WITNESSETH as follows:-

1. The Guarantor hereby covenants with the Employer that the Contractor will duly perform the obligations on the part of the Contractors contained in the Contract and that if the Contractors shall in any respect fail to execute the Contract or commit any breach of any of their obligations thereunder then the Guarantor will be responsible for and will indemnify and keep indemnified the Employer from and against all losses damages costs and expenses which may be suffered or incurred by it by reason of or arising directly or indirectly out of any default on the part of the Contractors in performing and observing the obligations on their part contained in the Contract.

In WITNESS whereof the Guarantor
have caused their Common Seal to
be hereunto affixed this day and
year first above written

THE COMMON SEAL OF

15

Chapter 3

PROGRESS AND SITE MEETINGS

Initial site or briefing meeting

As soon as practicable after the contract has been placed, the building team should meet. Although this initial meeting may take place on the site, it will more probably take place in either the architect's or contractor's office.

The manner in which this first meeting is conducted will greatly influence the success of the programme and succinct, clear direction from the chairman will be a strong inducement to a similar response from the others. Since at this stage the person having the most complete picture of the job is the architect, it seems logical that he should take the chair, at least at this first meeting. He will have discussed the arrangements for this meeting with the contractor beforehand, and it is suggested that the representatives of the following should attend:

employer
architect
quantity surveyor
structural consultant
services consultant
contractor
principal nominated sub-contractors
principal nominated suppliers
clerk of works

It is suggested that the agenda for this meeting should include the following matters:

1. Introduction of those attending.
2. Factors affecting the carrying out of the work.
3. Programme.
4. Sub-contracts and employer/sub-contractor agreements.
5. Communications.
6. Insurances (see chapter 2).
7. Procedure to be followed at subsequent meetings.

The introduction of those attending needs no elaboration, though it is more than just a formality as it establishes an initial contact between individuals who must work together in harmony if the contract is to run smoothly.

Factors affecting the carrying out of the works

These would normally be described fully in the contract documents, but may require emphasis and clarification at this initial meeting. They may include access to site; space availability; restrictions, such as hours of work and noise; building lines; buried services; site investigation and protection of the works, unfixed materials, adjoining buildings, work people and the general public.

16

Programme

The contractor should attend the initial site meeting with an outline programme for the work prepared in advance, the necessary basic information regarding delivery dates and construction times having been obtained from the principal nominated sub-contractors and suppliers. It is helpful to have this programme circulated to those attending before the meeting when it can then be properly considered and adjusted as necessary. Following this the contractor can then prepare the final programme and circulate it to all concerned.

The opportunity should be taken to stress the importance of adhering to dates once these have been agreed by the contractor and the nominated sub-contractors and suppliers. This applies also to dates agreed for the issue of architect's or consultant's drawings, where these have not already been prepared in the pre-contract stage. It is not uncommon for the contractor to indicate on his programme the latest dates by which he requires drawings, instructions for placing orders, schedules and other information from the architect and the latter must indicate at this stage whether he considers the proposed dates reasonable.

Sub-contracts

Many problems on building contracts arise from delay in the issue of instructions by the architect regarding nominated sub-contractors and suppliers and from difficulties in liaison between contractor and sub-contractors. It is advisable at this initial meeting, therefore, to clarify the position regarding all work covered by pre-contract sums in the bills of quantities.

It is essential for the smooth running of the contract that all nominations are made in adequate time for the work concerned to be phased into the contractor's programme without causing disruption. It should be made clear to the contractor that, once nominated, these sub-contractors and suppliers are his responsibility contractually.

The importance of proper sub-contract documentation should be stressed and this subject is dealt with in more detail in *Pre-Contract Practice*.

It is recommended in most cases that direct agreements between employer and sub-contractor are made, in which case the standard form should be used.

Communications

It is important at the initial site meeting that the procedure regarding architect's instructions should be made clear to all concerned. The matter is covered by clause 2 of the Conditions of Contract and is dealt with in chapter 5 of this book. Additional points which should be stressed at the initial site meeting will be found in the golden rules at the end of chapter 1.

Subsequent site meetings

This refers to formal site meetings and should not be confused with the architect's site inspections and the numerous meetings between the contractor and others, which may be necessary during the progress of the work. The frequency of site meetings will vary with the size and complexity of the contract, and according to the particular stage of the job and any difficulties encountered.

It is unlikely that these meetings at any stage would be at intervals of more than four weeks, and especially in the early stages they may well be held more frequently.

When considering the procedure to be followed, the following points should be borne in mind.

(a) *Notices to attend:*
   The architect should notify the quantity surveyor and consultants of the dates and times of site meetings, asking them to attend if their presence is required. It should be the responsibility of the contractor to call all sub-contractors' and suppliers' representatives whom he or the architect would like to be present.

(b) *Agenda:*
   The content of the agenda should be agreed before each meeting by the architect and the contractor. A standard form of agenda is useful, as a model and as an *aide memoire*. A typical agenda is shown in example 3.

(c) *Minutes:*
   Minutes should be impartially drafted and given the correct emphasis. Example 4 shows typical site meeting minutes.

On many large contracts it may be more convenient to divide the site meetings into two parts: the first under the chairmanship of the contractor will concern itself with the method of carrying out the work. It would be attended solely by the contractor's representatives and those of sub-contractors and suppliers. It will plan and organise the work on site. The second meeting will monitor progress and performance. It will be chaired by the architect and attended by the design team, the contractor, and such sub-contractors as are requested to attend. The object of this meeting would be to give the contractor the opportunity to raise questions on the drawings, specification, schedules and instructions issued; to request additional information and to report progress. Consideration of the value of people's time should be shown at all meetings; care should be taken not to call to meetings persons whose presence is not really necessary. It is important to realise that a badly run site meeting can be a serious waste of time to all, but if properly handled it can be a big saver of time. Furthermore, there is little doubt that these periodic meetings keep people up to the mark and impart a sense of urgency which is difficult in day-to-day correspondence.

The contractor should not regard the formal meetings as relieving him of the obligation to manage the job efficiently.

" ... an important aspect of site meetings ..."

EXAMPLE 3

AGENDA FOR SITE MEETING
to be held on (date)

Job *Aqua Products Ltd. New Factory*
Job No. *456*　　　　Date

---

1. Minutes of last meeting.
2. Matters arising and action taken.
3. Weather report since last meeting:　　　man/hours lost.
4. Labour force on site: at date of meeting by trades.
5. Questions on Architect's Instructions issued to date.
   Serial number of latest instruction (for verification). Verbal instructions requiring written confirmation.
6. Day Works: date of last sheet passed to Quantity Surveyors.
7. General Contractor's Progress Report.
8. General Contractor's report and questions on nominated sub-contractors:
   - (i) Mechanical services.
   - (ii) Electrical services.
   - (iii) Structural frame.
   - (iv) Others.
9. General Contractor's report and questions on nominated suppliers.
10. Comments from those in attendance.
11. Other items, AOB.
12. Date of next meeting.

Distribution:

Employer
Q.S.
Consultants
Contractor
Clerk of Works
Sub-Contractors &
Suppliers
Architect

EXAMPLE 4

MINUTES OF SITE MEETING
held on (date) *Memorandum No. 22*

Job *Aqua Products Ltd. New Factory*
Job No. *456*   Date

Present: Mr H.O. Waters   ..   Aqua Products Ltd
       Mr A. Gent   }   ..   W.E. Build & Co. Ltd
       Mr G. Foreman
       Mr. E. Steel   ..   R.C. Frame & Partners
       Mr P. Trapp   ..   Sanitary Supplies Ltd
       I.D.   }   ..   D. & D.
       O.E.
       Mr Peers   ..   Clerk of works

Serial	Item	Action
191	*Minutes of last meeting:* Agreed as correct.	
192	*Matters arising:* Ref. Serial 184 Mr Waters confirmed that his board had agreed not to move the Canteen.	
193	*Labour Force on Site:* Foreman 1 Labourers 16 Bricklayers 4	
194	*Delivery Materials:* Mr Gent reported that despite repeated telephone calls brick deliveries were still behind schedule from nominated suppliers. Architect to intervene. etc. etc. through agenda.	
205	*Steam Steriliser:* Mr Trapp produced working drawings of this and it was agreed that if drain cock was positioned on left instead of right it would fit in the recess. Mr Trapp to agree suitable position for steam inlet with Hotpipe Installations who will report to architect.	
206	*Door to Boiler House D.B.06:* Mr Waters said that his Works Engineer wished this to open on the opposite hand. Agreed. Architect to issue instruction.	
207	*Date of next meeting:* (date)	

Distribution: as agenda

Chapter 4

SITE SUPERVISION

The object of site supervision is primarily to ensure that the employer's requirements as expressed in the contract documents are correctly interpreted and that the problems which are bound to arise on even the smallest jobs, are satisfactorily resolved. Responsibility for supervision is shared between the builder and the architect. The latter is under an obligation to his client under the terms of his engagement and the former is bound by the conditions of his contract to complete the work in a certain time and to a specified standard, which would not be possible without a degree of supervision.

The nature and extent of the supervisory arrangements will depend on the size and complexity of the works. On a small contract for example, the builder may be able to rely on a competent general foreman, while on larger contracts a number of foremen and assistants may be required working under a site agent, if the job is to be properly organised. Similarly the architect may supervise a small contract adequately by periodic visits, whereas one or more clerks of works may be needed and possibly a resident architect, on large and complex buildings. In this chapter we are assuming that there will be a clerk of works acting, as the contract provides, 'as inspector on behalf of the employer under the directions of the architect'.

We are concerned with site supervision by the architect and this can be considered under the following heads:

1. Formal site meetings
2. Routine site inspections
3. Records and reports
4. Samples and testing

Site meetings have been dealt with in the preceding chapter. The remaining headings, however, do call for some further comment.

Routine site inspections

The architect will normally have more time to inspect the work when making routine inspections than on those occasions when a formal site meeting is held. The frequency of these inspections will obviously depend on the size and complexity of the work and the speed of the progress being made. It will also depend on whether or not a clerk of works or a resident architect is engaged.

As a matter of courtesy the architect should make his presence on the site known to the clerk of works and the foreman in charge who will normally accompany him around the job.

The architect should never give instructions to a workman direct. The general foreman is the only man on the site with authority under the contract to act upon architect's instructions. All instructions should be confirmed in writing after the visit as set out in chapter 5.

SITE SUPERVISION

The Health and Safety at Work Act 1974 imposes certain legal responsibilities upon the contractor and employer. Where the possession of the site is vested in the contractor the primary liability for health and safety rests with him and the architect should ensure that these responsibilities are met. Where the site is in the possession of the employer, or jointly with the contractor, both the employer and the contractor are responsible for the health and safety of the workforce and other persons on site. The contractor, as the expert, is responsible for the plant. Recommendations contained in BS 5306:Part 1:1976 Code of Practice for Fire Extinguishing Installations and Equipment on Premises should also be observed, a point which might have been covered in the bills of quantities.

When making a site inspection it is easy to be distracted and to overlook items which require attention. It is a good plan, therefore, to list in advance particular points to be looked at and any special reason for doing so. For this purpose a standard check-list is helpful as it serves as a useful *aide memoire*. The contents of such a list must be of a rather general nature and it can then be amplified or adapted for each job according to the type of work and form of construction involved. A typical standard check-list is given in example 5.

Records and reports

Where a clerk of works is employed, the architect should receive weekly reports from the site, covering:

(a) Number of men employed in the various trades.
(b) State of the weather and particulars of time lost due to exceptionally inclement weather.
(c) Principal deliveries of materials and particulars of any shortages.
(d) Plant on the site.
(e) Particulars of any drawings or other information required.
(f) Visitors to the site.
(g) General progress in relation to the programme.
(h) Any other matters affecting the smooth running of the contract.

A standard form of report is usually provided by the architect and a typical one is shown in example 6.

The weekly report is valuable in keeping the architect fully informed of day-to-day progress, and also constitutes a useful record for reference if disputes arise at a later date. The weekly report should be compiled from the diary of the clerk of works. This diary should be provided by the architect at the commencement of the job and should be returned to him on completion. In it should be recorded daily all matters affecting the contract.

A copy of the builder's programme should be kept in the office of the clerk of works, and every week the actual progress should be checked against this programme.

It is the job of the clerk of works to keep records of any departures from the working drawings which may be found necessary in order that, on completion, the architect has all the information necessary to enable him to issue to the employer an accurate set of drawings of the finished building. These records are particularly important where the work is to be concealed, as for example foundations, the depth of which may vary from that shown on the original working drawings.

Progress photographs of the work also form valuable records if taken regularly.

This is probably best arranged in conjunction with the contractor so that both he and the architect can have the benefit of them.

Samples and testing

The architect may call for samples of various components and materials required in the building to be submitted for approval in order that he can satisfy himself of their construction or quality and that they meet the requirements of the client and, where applicable, the local planning authorities.

The following is an indication of some of the items of which samples would normally be required:

(a) Facing bricks, artificial or natural stone, precast concrete, marble, terrazzo, slates or roofing tiles.

(b) Joinery, mouldings, timber, wall or flooring tiles, cement glaze or other decorative finishes.

(c) Plumbing components, sanitary goods, ironmongery, electrical fittings, etc.

In addition to samples of individual components or materials, the architect will often require sample panels prepared on the site to enable him to judge the effect of materials in the positions in which they will be used. Panels of facing bricks are an example of this.

It is quite normal to require laboratory tests of basic materials such as concrete. The crushing strength of bricks may also be tested in a laboratory, though, unless the design requirements are at all stringent, a certificate from the manufacturers giving their characteristics may suffice. The testing of concrete should be carried out on a regular basis and cubes should be cast from each main batch of concrete, carefully labelled and identified. The tests themselves should be carried out by an approved laboratory and the test reports submitted by the contractor to the architect or structural engineer.

British Standard Specifications and Codes of Practice are specified for many building materials, components and processes, and in carrying out tests it is essential to refer to the appropriate standard or code to ensure that the requirements are complied with. In addition the British Standards Institution lays down acceptable tolerances for manufactured goods, and copies of the relevant standards and codes should always be kept by the clerk of works on the site.

EXAMPLE 5

STANDARD CHECK-LIST FOR SITE INSPECTIONS

This list should be amplified or adapted according to the nature of the job under supervision and may serve architect or engineer. Some of the items should be inspected jointly with other consultants.

1. General

In all cases check that the work complies with the drawings and specification, with the latest requirements of the statutory undertakers and with the building regulations.

2. Preliminary works

(a) Siting of workmen's canteens and builder's offices, etc.
(b) Removal of top soil and location of spoil heaps.
(c) Perimeter fencing or hoardings.
(d) Provision for protection of rights of way.
(e) Protection of trees and other special site features.
(f) Party wall agreements and protection of adjoining property.
(g) Protection of materials on site.
(h) Site security generally.
(i) Suitability and siting of clerk of works or site architect's office.
(j) Ensure that drawings, bills of quantities and other information is complete.
(k) Agree bench mark or level pegs.
(l) Agree setting out.

3. Demolition

(a) Extent
(b) Adequacy of shoring.
(c) Burning on site.
(d) Preservation of certain materials and special items.

4. Excavation and foundations

(a) Widths of trenches.
(b) Depths of excavations.
(c) Nature of ground in relation to trial hole report.
(d) Stability and timbering of excavations.
(e) Pumping arrangements.
(f) Risk to adjoining property or general public.
(g) Quality of concrete and thickness of beds.
(h) Suitability of hardcore (freedom from rubbish).
(i) Quality of sand and ballast (freedom from loam and correct grading).
(j) Damp-proof membranes or asphalt tanking.
(k) Ducts, drains or services under building.
(l) Correct placing of reinforcement, including diameter, bending and spacing of bars.
(m) Consolidation of backfilling, particularly suitability of material used for backfilling.
(n) Ascertain depths of piles and driving conditions in case of piled foundations.

EXAMPLE 5 *(cont.)*

5. Drainage

(a) Depths of inverts and gradients of falls.
(b) Timbering of trenches.
(c) Thickness of concrete bed and jointing of pipes.
(d) Quality of bricks for manholes and rendering thereto.
(e) Testing of drains and manholes (water test), etc.

6. Brickwork, blockwork and concrete masonry

(a) Approve sample panels of facings and fairface work.
(b) Quality and colour of mortar and pointing.
(c) Test report on crushing strength where necessary.
(d) BS certificates on load-bearing blocks.
(e) Silt test on sand.
(f) Position and type of wall ties and inspect cavities to external walls to ensure cavities clean above DPC's and wall ties clean.
(g) Correct setting-out and maintenance of regular vertical and horizontal joints.
(h) Solid bedding to horizontal and vertical joints.
(i) Type and quality of DPC's and correct placing.
(j) Correct setting-out and fixings for door frames, windows, etc.
(k) Bedding and levels of lintels over openings.
(l) Position of fixing blocks, etc.
(m) Expansion joints.

7. In-situ concrete

(a) Setting out and stability of shuttering.
(b) Correct shuttering to achieve type of finish specified.
(c) Setting out of reinforcement, fixings, holes and water bars.
(d) Mix and correct procedure of taking test cubes.
(e) Curing of concrete and striking of shuttering.

8. Precast concrete

(a) Size and shape of units.
(b) Finish.
(c) Position of fixings, holes, etc.
(d) Damage in transit and erection.
(e) Neoprene strips, water bars, etc.

9. Carpentry and joinery

(a) Freedom from loose knots, shakes, sapwood, insect attack, etc.
(b) Dimensions within permissible tolerances.
(c) Application of timber preservatives and primers.
(d) Storage and stacking and protection from weather.
(e) Jointing, bolting, spiking and notching of carpenter's timber.
(f) Spacing of floor and ceiling joints and position of trimmers.
(g) Spacing of battens, position of noggings.
(h) Weather throatings and hardwood cills to doors and windows, etc.
(i) Jointing, machining and finish of manufactured joinery.

EXAMPLE 5 *(cont.)*

10. Roofing

  (a) Pitch of roof.
  (b) Spacing of rafters and tile battens.
  (c) Approval of underfelt.
  (d) Approval of roofing tiles and nailing as specified.
  (e) Pointing to verges.
  (f) Bedding of ridges, etc.
  (g) Falls to outlets for flat roofs.
  (h) Thickness of insulation under finish.
  (i) Chasing of walls and parapets to tuck in asphalt.
  (j) Pointing above skirtings and flashings.
  (k) Fixing of drips to external edges and finish of asphalt thereto.
  (l) Weight of lead to lead roofs and correct formation of flashings, etc.

11. Cladding

  (a) Vapour barriers and insulation.
  (b) Regularity of grounds for sheet materials.
  (c) Location and quality of fixings (cleats, bolts, nails, etc.).
  (d) Laps, tolerances, and positions of joints.
  (e) Setting-out and jointing of mullions and rails.
  (f) Glass sizes, tolerances, spacers and fixing.
  (g) Glazing compounds.
  (h) Handling and protection of panel materials (metal, glass and GRP).
  (i) Specification and application of mastic.
  (j) Flashings, edge trims and weather drips.
  (k) Entry and egress of moisture.
  (l) Prevention of electrolytic action.
  (m) Specification of mortar bedding and pointing.
  (n) Location and type of movement joints (brick and tile claddings).

12. Steel work

  (a) Sizes of steel.
  (b) Rivets and welding.
  (c) Position of steels.
  (d) Plumbing, squaring and levelling of steel frame.
  (e) Priming and protection.

13. Metal work

  (a) Sizes and spacing of members.
  (b) Galvanising or rustproofing, if specified.
  (c) Connections between units to be similarly protected.
  (d) Stability of supports, including caulking or plugging.
  (e) Isolation from corrosive materials, etc.

14. Plumbing and sanitary goods

  (a) Inspect sanitary goods to ensure freedom from cracks or deformities.
  (b) Protection against frost.

EXAMPLE 5 *(cont.)*

   (c)   Location and fixing of stack pipes.
   (d)   Falls to waste branches.
   (e)   Use of traps.
   (f)   Jointing of pipes.
   (g)   Smoke and/or water tests.
   (h)   Location and accessibility of valves, stop-cocks.
   (i)   Drain down-cocks at lowest point.
   (j)   Access to traps and rodding eyes.

15. Heating, hot water and ventilation installations

   (a)   Type of boiler, calorifier, fans, etc, as specified.
   (b)   Type of pipes.
   (c)   Position and type of stop valves.
   (d)   Position of pipe runs and ventilation trunking.
   (e)   Insulation of pipe work.
   (f)   Identification and labelling of pipes, valves, etc. and directions of flow.

16. Electrical installation

   (a)   Approval of components.
   (b)   Switches, fuses, cables, etc., against specification.
   (c)   Position of heating, lighting and switch points as compared with drawings.
   (d)   Earthing of installation.
   (e)   Lightning conductor installation.
   (f)   Runs of cables and quality of connections, etc.
   (g)   Labelling and identification of switchgear, etc.

17. Specialist installations

   (a)   Specialist drawings on site.
   (b)   Drawings of builders work in connection with installation.
   (c)   Special statutory regulations and controls.
   (d)   Unforeseen changes in design of special equipment.
   (e)   Power and plant to be provided during installation.
   (f)   Access for equipment and provision of adequate working space.
   (g)   Temporary support, loading on structure, lifting tackle, etc.
   (h)   Provision of services.
   (i)   Provision of correct temperature, humidity and ventilation during installation.
   (j)   Attendance on site and correct sequence of work.
   (k)   Accuracy, size and positions of holes, levels, plumb lines, and tolerances generally.
   (l)   Correct type and setting-out of fixings.
   (m) Junctions with surrounding finishes.
   (n)   Safety – operatives in confined spaces, contractor's workforce and the public. (Volatile and noxious gases, radiation, noise, etc.).

18. Pacing and floor tiling

   (a)   Approve materials.

EXAMPLE 5 *(cont.)*

(b) Quality of screeds to receive flooring.
(c) Junctions of differing floor finishes.
(d) Regularity of finish.
(e) Falls to gulleys, etc.
(f) Skirtings and coves.
(g) Non-slip surfaces, if specified, etc.

19. Plastering

(a) Storage of material.
(b) Correct mix.
(c) Preparation of surface.
(d) True surfaces and arrises (including angle and casing heads).
(e) Fixing of laths or plaster board.
(f) Filling and scrimming of joints in plaster board.
(g) Bonding plaster on concrete or adequate hacking.
(h) Wall tiling, regularity of joints.
(i) Rounded edge-tiles on external angles.

20. Suspended ceilings

(a) Type of suspension and tile.
(b) Height of ceiling and correct setting-out.
(c) Position of light fittings, ventilation grilles, etc.
(d) Access panels.
(e) Finish for curtains, blinds, etc.

21. Glazing

(a) Quality of glass and freedom from defects.
(b) Correct type and/or thickness.
(c) Size of sheets to allow fractional movement in frames.
(d) Depth of rebates.
(e) Glazing compound, fixing of glazing beads, etc.

22. Painting and decorating

(a) Approval of material being used.
(b) Storage of material safe from frost.
(c) Preparation of surfaces and freedom from damp.
(d) Specified coats.
(e) Take sample from painter's can for test to check against over-thinning.
(f) Inspect surfaces partly concealed, viz insides of eaves, gutters.
(g) Finished work – freedom from runs, brush marks, etc.
(h) Opacity of finish, etc.

23. Cleaning down and handing over

(a) Windows cleaned and floors scrubbed.
(b) Floors free from paint spots.
(c) Sanitary goods washed and flushed.
(d) Painted surfaces immaculate.

EXAMPLE 5 *(cont.)*

(e) Doors correctly fitted, windows not binding or rattling.
(f) Ironmongery complete and locks and latches operating correctly.
(g) Correct number of keys.
(h) Floor or overhead springs correctly adjusted.
(i) Connection of services, provision of meters, etc.
(j) Commissioning of all mechanical engineering plant, balancing of air-conditioning, etc.
(k) Plant maintenance manuals, plant room service diagrams, etc.
(l) Operation of security, communication and fire protection systems.

" *possibly a resident architect* "

EXAMPLE 6

Report No. ....

DRAW & DRAW

Date ....

CLERK OF WORKS REPORT

Job .... Job No. ....

Contractor ....

Contract period .... weeks from .... Construction week No. ....

Extension .... Anticipated completion date ....

	WORKMEN EMPLOYED							STOPPAGES (in hours)								
	Mon.	Tues.	Wed.	Thurs.	Fri.	Sat.			Mon.	Tues.	Wed.	Thur.	Fri.	Sat.	TOTAL for WEEK	TOTAL TO DATE
Foreman								Inclement weather								
Timekeeper								Frost								
Labourers								Holidays								
Bricklayers								Other causes								
Masons								TOTAL								
Carpenters								DELAYS state cause								
Tilers and Slaters																
Joiners																
Plasterers																
Smiths																
Plumbers																
Painters																
Electricians																
Heating Engineers																
Asphalters																
TOTALS																

PLANT & MATERIALS ON SITE	DRAWINGS & INFORMATION RECEIVED	VISITORS

PLANT & MATERIAL SHORTAGES	DRAWINGS & INFORMATION REQUIRED	

EXAMPLE 6 *(cont.)*

Report on work in hand and progress

(fold here)

The whole of the work executed during the past week is satisfactory.

....
Clerk of Works

Draw & Draw
13 Corb's Buildings,
London, SW1 3BS

Examined by

....

32

Chapter 5

INSTRUCTIONS AND VARIATIONS

If the procedure set out in *Pre-Contract Practice* is followed it should be possible for complete sets of drawings, together with specification notes and nominated sub-contractors' and suppliers' estimates to be available to the quantity surveyor, who will then be in a position to prepare fully described and accurate bills of quantities which can be annotated at a later stage. This in turn will mean that immediately the contract is placed the contractor can be handed all the necessary information to build the project in hand.

Architect's instructions

Despite this complete planning and documentation, however, it will probably be necessary from time to time for the architect to issue further drawings, details and instructions which are collectively known as 'Architect's Instructions'. The conditions of contract lay down those matters in connection with which the architect is empowered to issue such instructions, and as the contractor is entitled under clause 2 (2) to question the architect's right to issue any particular instruction, it is as well to be clear as to which clauses give him the authority. They are as follows:

Clause 1 (2)   Discrepancies in documents.
Clause 4 (1)   Compliance with acts of parliament, bye-laws, and other regulations.
Clause 5   Levels and setting-out.
Clause 6 (3)   Opening up work for inspection.
Clause 6 (4)   Removal of work, materials or goods not complying with the contract.
Clause 6 (5)   Dismissal of any person employed on the works.
Clause 11 (1) Variations in the design, quality or quantity of the work.
Clause 11 (3) Expenditure of prime cost and provisional sums.
Clause 15 (3) Making good defects.
Clause 21 (2) Postponement of the execution of any work.
Clause 27   Nominated sub-contractors' work.
Clause 28   Nominated suppliers' work.
Clause 32 (2) Protection of the work in the event of war.
Clause 33 (1) Action in the event of war damage.
Clause 34 (2) Antiquities.

The procedure for the issue of instructions is set out in clause 2 (3) and this may be summarised as follows:

1. An instruction issued by the architect must be in writing.
2. An oral instruction is not effective unless it is confirmed by the contractor or architect within seven days. If confirmed by the contractor within the stated

period and the architect does not dissent then it is deemed to be an Architect's Instruction, and

3. The instruction is effective from the date of the issue of the Architect's Instruction or the expiration of the seven-day period referred to above, but

4. If neither the architect nor the contractor confirm any oral instructions, but the contractor still carries out the work in question as a matter of goodwill, then the architect can at any time up to the issue of the final certificate confirm the oral instructions in writing; these instructions should then be effective from the date of the written confirmation.

It is important to note here that clause 10 provides that if the clerk of works issues any directions to the contractor or to his foreman, such directions are only effective if they are in respect of matters about which the architect is empowered to issue instructions, and if they are confirmed by the architect within two working days, not, it will be noted, within seven days as provided for confirmation of the architect's own verbal instructions.

All instructions from the architect to the contractor should be issued, or confirmed, on a standard form. Such a form, shown in example 7, is published by RIBA Publications Ltd, but many other forms, containing the same essential features, have been produced for specific jobs or architectural offices. The use of such forms has several advantages, not least being the saving in work in issuing such instructions and the fact that they are immediately recognisable to all parties to the contract.

It contributes to the smooth running of the contract if verbal instructions given by the architect during site visits or directions given by the clerk of works are recorded in a duplicate book or on a duplicate pad of site orders which can be signed at the time and subsequently confirmed by an instruction as set out above.

It is essential that instructions should be clear and precise, and where revised drawings are issued, the revision should be specifically referred to.

Instructions emanating from consultants should be passed to the architect for confirmation by Architect's Instructions.

Copies of Architect's Instructions should be distributed as follows:

general contractor (2 copies)
clerk of works
quantity surveyor
consultant (if concerned).

It should be stressed at the initial site meeting to all concerned that no adjustment will be made to the contract sum unless the matter is covered by an Architect's Instruction in accordance with the terms of the contract.

Variations

Before considering those instructions which involve variations it might be useful to define what is a variation. Clause 11 (2) states:

The term 'variation' as used in these Conditions means the alteration or modification of the design, quality or quantity of the Works as shown upon the Contract Drawings and described by or referred to in the Contract Bills, and includes the addition, omission or substitution of any work, the alteration of the kind or standard of any of the materials or goods to be used in the Works, and the removal from the site of any work materials or goods executed or brought thereon by the Contractor for the purposes of the Works other than work materials or goods which are not in accordance with this Contract.

The Architect's Instruction will describe the varied work, state any item or items to be omitted, and will record any new or amended drawings which are to be worked to. If the instruction involves the adjustment of prime cost sums, particulars must be given of the estimate which is to be accepted, stating the date of the quotation and the reference number as well as the total value of the proposed accepted estimate.

While we are not concerned in this chapter with the preparation of the final account, we do set out here the basic rules for the valuation of variations. These are laid down in clause 11 (4) of the conditions of contract which states that they shall be measured and valued by the quantity surveyor, who shall give the contractor the opportunity of being present and of taking such notes and measurements as he may require, unless the matter is covered by a tender submitted by the contractor, under clause 27(g), and accepted by the architect as a lump sum. The valuation made by the quantity surveyor is required to be made in accordance with the following rules:

(a) Where the work is of a similar nature and executed under similar conditions to that in the main contract, then the measured quantities of the variation will be priced at rates contained in the contract bills.

(b) Where, however, the work is not of a similar nature nor executed under similar conditions to that contemplated under the terms of the contract, then the rates contained in the contract bills shall form the basis of a price to be agreed with the contractor as far as is reasonable. If the work contained in the variation is totally different from anything contained in the contract then a fair valuation will be made by the quantity surveyor for agreement with the contractor.

(c) Where it is impossible by the normal methods of measurement or price build-up, to fairly represent the cost of the work carried out, then, unless otherwise agreed, the work shall be allowed at daywork rates at the prices ruling at the date the work is actually carried out as follows:

    (i) The prime cost of the work calculated in accordance with the 'Definition of Prime Cost of Daywork carried out under a Building Contract' issued by the RICS and the NFBTE and current at the 'date of tender' together with percentage additions to each section of the prime cost at the rates set out by the contractor in the contract bills and recorded in the appendix to the conditions of contract, or

    (ii) Where work is in the province of any specialist trade, and where the RICS and the appropriate body representing the employers in that trade have agreed and issued a definition of prime cost of daywork, the contractor shall be allowed the prime cost of such work calculated in accordance with that definition current at the 'date of tender' together with percentage additions as previously.

Although (i) and (ii) above represent the rules for daywork rates in the contract, an alternative is sometimes required. This arises when the contractor is required to quote daywork rates in the tender documents. In this case the contract clauses have to be amended, a practice which is not recommended.

In every case stated above the daywork sheets must be submitted to the architect not later than the week following that in which the work was carried out. The architect or his authorized representative, usually the clerk of works, can then within a reasonable period of time certify the accuracy of the hours recorded and the materials used and, if satisfied, can sign the sheets as a true record of the time and materials used. The daywork sheets will then be passed to the quantity surveyor who will satisfy himself that the labour, materials and plant recorded on them are reasonable for the work involved. He will also, of course, check the prices and arithmetic.

It is advisable that all daywork sheets be serially numbered, state the date when the work was carried out, specify the daily time spent on the work set against each operative's name and list the materials and plant used. The architect should check that he has issued the necessary instruction covering the work (a signed daywork sheet does not constitute an instruction) and reference to this instruction should be made on the daywork sheets concerned.

(d) All omissions from the contract are valued at the rates contained in the contract bills unless the omissions are of such an extensive nature that they substantially vary the contract conditions under which the remaining work must be carried out, when the rates for the remaining work are valued as under (b) above.

The conditions of contract clearly state that interim valuations shall account for any costs due to variations or adjustment of provisional sums and it is, therefore, important that the quantity surveyor keeps up-to-date with the measurement and valuation of authorized variations.

From time to time instructions are issued by the architect which, when measured and valued using the rules set out above, involve the contractor in a direct loss or expense beyond that which could reasonably be contemplated under the terms of the contract. The contractor can, if such occasion arises, apply to the architect for the amount of this loss to be ascertained and if the architect agrees in principle then the amount of this loss or expense will be added to the contract sum. If the ascertained loss occurs during the course of the contract, the amount may be included in certificate valuations.

Cost control

Cost control may be defined as the controlling measures necessary to ensure that the authorized cost of the project is not exceeded. It is a continuing process following the cost planning and cost control exercised during the design period (chapter II of *Pre-Contract Practice*).

Normally the authorized cost will be represented by the contract sum. However, there may be occasions when the sum can be varied while construction is taking place. For example, a client building speculatively may find that his tenant is prepared to pay more for a particular facility, in which case he will give instructions for this to be assessed and, if implemented, an adjustment will be made to the authorized cost.

One essential point to establish at the outset is the extent to which the client requires cost control. Both architect and quantity surveyor should obtain the client's instructions on this point. On the one hand he may issue an overall instruction that on no account must the authorized sum be exceeded; alternatively, he may require the cost to be carefully monitored throughout while giving over-riding priority to the quality of the building. In this connection it is good practice to clarify the purpose of the contingency sum with the client at the outset of the job. Generally the contingency sum should only be used to cover the cost of extra work which could not reasonably have been foreseen at the design stage (e.g. extra work below ground level). It should not be used for design alterations, except with the prior approval of the client.

INSTRUCTIONS AND VARIATIONS

To maintain cost control, it is necessary for the value of all possible variations to be assessed before instructions are issued so that their effect may be taken into account. This process needs extremely close liaison between architect and quantity surveyor and the other consultants. It demands the quantity surveyor's attendance at all relevant meetings, including site meetings, and the submission to him of copies of all correspondence which may have cost implications. Where time allows, it is a useful discipline for all proposed instructions to be discussed with the quantity surveyor for pricing, prior to their formal issue. This allows consideration to be given to the cost effect of an instruction before the expenditure is committed. It is also wise for the architect to look ahead and make early decisions on such matters as expenditure against provisional and prime cost sums and the likelihood of variations in the later stages.

The necessity for strict cost control does not eliminate the need for continuing cost studies in areas of construction which have not been finally detailed. If this is done effectively the likelihood of having to draw on the contingency sum is lessened. Indeed the contingency provision can even be built up to cope with unforeseen variations and if none occur a saving will ultimately be made for the client against the authorized cost.

The evaluation of possible variations and the likely outcome of expenditure to be set against prime cost and provisional sums should not preclude looking at legitimate claims which might be made by the contractor and taking these into account early on in forecasting final cost.

Whether full cost control is required or monitoring of costs, it will be necessary for the quantity surveyor to produce monthly forecasts of final expenditure. In these he should not only take into account formal Architect's Instructions, but also known extras or savings. For example, if the district surveyor or fire officer has indicated that he will be making certain requirements that have not been taken into account in the contract, then the quantity surveyor should include an assessment of the effects of these pending the formal instructions from the architect.

The monthly forecasts of final expenditure should take into account the amount of the contingency sum still remaining and consideration should be given to the adequacy of any such amount in the circumstances. In the early stages of the work most of the contingency sum, if it remains unspent, should still be included, but as the contract progresses it can be reduced as the risk of unforeseen extras diminishes. In the event of the contingency sum being spent in the early stages, consideration will have to be given to including a further contingency allowance in cost reports and notifying the client accordingly.

On large projects, it may well be inappropriate for monthly statements to be made and quarterly will suffice.

Where specialist engineering works are supervised by a consulting engineer, instructions, although emanating from the engineer, will be issued by the architect. Cost control, preferably before the issue of these instructions is just as important as with any other instructions and close liaison is essential so that all parties know the full implications of the costs identified.

An example of a financial report is given in example 8.

37

" ... where ... work is of a similar nature ... "

EXAMPLE 7

Architect's name and address	Draw & Draw, Chartered Architects, 13 Corb's Buildings, London, SW1 3BS 01-930 0001		

Architect's Instruction

Works	New Factory – Aqua Products Ltd
situate at	Newtown

To contractor	W.E. Build & Co. Ltd	**Instruction no.**	25
Under the terms of the Contract		**Date**	20th July 1978

dated

I/We issue the following instructions. Where applicable the contract sum will be adjusted in accordance with the terms of the relevant Condition.

For office use: Approx costs

Instructions	£ omit	£ add
1. <u>Flush doors</u>		
<u>Omit</u> P.C. Sum of £1,750 (B.Q. item 70/K) for supply of flush doors.	*	
<u>Add</u> Place your order for the supply of flush doors with Wood Doors Ltd, Pinewood, Acton in accordance with their quotation ref. S/739 dated 11th January 1978 in the sum of £1,731.50, including 5% cash discount (copy enclosed).		*
2. <u>Tile splashbacks</u>		
Change specification of tile splashbacks from two courses 150 mm tiles to three courses of 100 mm tiles. (Drwg 39 revision C enclosed.)		*
3. <u>Blank opening G 10</u>		
Increase width of blank opening G 10 in kitchen from 1200 mm to 1500 mm. (Note – alteration to existing blockwork to be recorded on daywork – lintel not yet delivered to site.)		*

Office reference   **Signed**

Architect/Supervising officer

Notes

* Approximate costing for cost control purposes may be shown on appropriate copies.

Amount of contract sum £	
± Approximate value of previous instructions £	_____
£	
± Approximate value of this instruction £	_____
Approximate adjusted total £	

To Contractor ☐	Copies to Employer ☐	Quantity surveyor ☐	Clerk of works ☐	Structural consultant ☐
Heating consultant ☐	Electrical consultant ☐	☐	☐	Architect's file ☐

© 1967 RIBA

EXAMPLE 8

Quantity Surveyor's Cost Report

Measures & Partners,
Chartered Quantity Surveyors,
1 Dims Place,
London, SW1 5AB

Contract: Factory
    Aqua Products Ltd.
Ref: 456
Financial Report No: 14

		£
1. Amount of Contract		360,427
2. Alteration to Brief	Add/~~Omit~~	2,000
		362,427
3. Omit Contingencies		8,915
		353,512
4. Variations as Appendix	Add/~~Omit~~	2,241
		355,753
5. Add allowance for Contingencies for remainder of Contract		1,000
6. ESTIMATED FINAL COST (excluding fluctuations)		356,753
7. Add allowance for fluctuations		30,500
8. ESTIMATED TOTAL FINAL COST		£387,253

Date: Signed: ....

EXAMPLE 8 *(cont.)*

FINANCIAL REPORT No. 14   Appendix

FACTORY, AQUA PRODUCTS LTD

Summary of Variations	Savings £	Extras £
Architect's Instructions Nos. 1–43 as previously reported	—	2,300
A.I. No. 44 Additional steel beam to lift motor room	—	75
A.I. No. 45 Omission of emulsion paint to stores	87	—
A.I. No. 46 Hardwood strip flooring in area G.4	—	314
Adjustment of provisional quantities	361	—
	448	2,689
		448
Variations – Net Adjustment	Add	£2,241

41

This is to
certify that
J. ARRIS
ARIBA
has qualified
as a
Registered
Plumber

"certificates"

Chapter 6

INTERIM CERTIFICATES

Clause 30 of the conditions of contract sets out the procedure for payment to the contractor.

Obligations

The obligations of the parties to the contract and of the employer's consultants are briefly as follows:

The employer

As soon as an architect's certificate is issued the employer incurs a debt which must be paid to the contractor within 14 days of the date on which the contractor presents the certificate for payment. If the employer fails to honour an architect's certificate, the contractor is empowered, under clause 26, to determine the contract, and can start proceedings in the normal way for recovery of the debt. The employer may, however, stay any proceedings for recovery of the debt by giving notice of arbitration if he disagrees with the architect's certificate. As explained in chapter 8 this is one of the matters which can be dealt with by arbitration before the practical completion of the works.

The architect

The architect must issue interim certificates at the period stated in the appendix to the conditions of contract and when further amounts become due after he has issued the Certificate of Practical Completion. The conditions state that to arrive at the amount due in interim certificates, the architect may, if he considers them necessary, request the quantity surveyor to prepare interim valuations. This is the normal procedure, except where previous stage payments have been agreed. If a quantity surveyor does not for any reason produce an interim valuation prior to any date for the issue of an interim certificate, the architect must still under the terms of the contract issue a certificate.

The architect is legally responsible for the accuracy of his certificate as he is regarded as acting as a specialist or expert and not as an arbitrator in granting of certificates (*Sutcliffe* v *Thackrah* 1974). He must also remain independent in the issuing of certificates so as to be fair to both parties (*Hickman* v *Roberts* 1913).

The quantity surveyor

Interim valuations for the purpose of ascertaining the amount to be stated as due in an interim certificate are to be prepared whenever the architect considers these valuations to be necessary. Clause 30 does not specifically state that the quantity surveyor should prepare these interim valuations but it is customary for him to do so.

The contractor

The contractor is under no obligation under the contract to assist in any way in the preparation of interim valuations or certificates. It is the architect's responsibility to assess the amount due and to issue the interim certificate and it is the employer's responsibility to make payment to the contractor within the fourteen-day period. In practice, however, it is customary for the contractor to co-operate with the quantity surveyor in the preparation of certificate valuations and this is clearly a sensible and satisfactory procedure.

Architect's interim certificate

In the ordinary course of events the architect will receive from the quantity surveyor a valuation on which he will base his interim certificate. This certificate must state:
1. The total value of the work *properly executed*. The architect is within his powers if he withholds payment in respect of work not properly executed.
2. The total value of the materials and goods delivered to or adjacent to the works.
    The last sentence of clause 30 (2) is important. The materials and goods must have been delivered to or adjacent to the works not later than seven days before the date of the certificate and must not have been brought on to the site prematurely. For example, unless there was some prior agreement on the matter the architect could rightly withhold payment for, say, joinery fitments brought on to the site when site stripping was still in progress. Although, once materials and goods are certified and paid for, the contractor remains responsible for loss or damage to them, they become the employer's property and must not be removed from the works without his authority. They must also be 'adequately protected' and the architect can refuse to include the value of any materials and goods which he does not consider to be properly protected 'against weather or other casualties'.
    Questions do arise from time to time regarding payment for materials and goods which have been prepared or manufactured for a contract and which have to be stored away from the site, perhaps at the supplier's works, until it is convenient for them to be delivered. Clause 30 of the conditions of contract cater for this situation by sub-clause 2(A). The operation of this clause is entirely at the architect's discretion, and if the circumstances of a contract are such that payment for off-site goods and materials is likely to be called for the matter should be considered at an early stage so that, when any such payments become due, they can be dealt with expeditiously. The clause sets out in detail the conditions which must be fulfilled before these payments can be approved. If the architect decides to use his discretion in this matter, and if the conditions have been fulfilled, then the value of these off-site goods and materials must also be included in the certificate.
3. Amount deducted for retention by the employer.
4. Any instalments previously paid.
    The use of a standard form of certificate is recommended and the current form issued by the RIBA is reproduced in example 10.
    In the Group's view there is much to be said for using a two-part form in which the first part consists of the quantity surveyor's valuation and the second part an endorsement for completion by the architect certifying the payment in accordance with the contract. Such a form is shown in example 11. Its use eliminates

unnecessary typing and reduces the possibility of errors in transferring figures.

In accordance with clauses 3 (8) and 30 (1), the interim certificate is issued to the contractor who presents it to the employer for payment. A copy should also, of course, be sent to the quantity surveyor. It might be noted here that this is one matter in which the Local Authority's edition of the contract differs from the private edition. In the former all certificates are issued direct to the employer.

Clause 27(b) of the contract requires the architect to 'direct the contractor as to the total value of the work, materials or goods executed or supplied by a nominated sub-contractor included in the calculation of the amount stated as due in any certificate under clause 30 of these conditions and shall forthwith inform the nominated sub-contractor in writing of the amount of the said total value'.

For this purpose a standard form of notification is published by the RIBA and is reproduced in example 12. As an alternative some firms prefer their own form incorporating a tear-off slip which the sub-contractor can return confirming that he has received payment due to him. A typical form of this type is shown in example 13.

Quantity surveyor's interim valuations

There is no obligation in the contract on the part of the quantity surveyor to advise the contractor of the amount he is recommending to the architect for payment but, since the make-up of the quantity surveyor's valuation will usually include more detail than is required in the architect's certificate, and since as previously stated the valuations, in practice, are almost invariably agreed with the contractor before presentation to the architect, it is desirable for the quantity surveyor to send a copy of his valuation to the contractor at the same time as he sends it to the architect.

Many quantity surveyors use the RICS standard form for certificate valuations in which the figures are set out in a similar manner to architect's certificate (example 9).

The gross value of work executed and materials delivered to, or adjacent to the site, together with any off-site goods and materials for which payment has been authorized, should include any such work or materials authorized as variations.

Fluctuations

No directions are given as to time of payment for increased costs or allowance for decreased costs in clause 31(A) to (E). It is good practice, however, for the quantity surveyor to make allowance in interim valuations for fluctuations where applicable, based on accurate records presented by the contractor.

If clauses 31(A) to (E) are deleted in the contract and clause 31(F) applies, then directions are clearly set down as to payment. Each certificate is to allow for the effect of the application of the NEDO Price Adjustment Formula. Effectively therefore clause 31(F) means that the quantity surveyor must prepare an interim valuation before the issue of each interim certificate.

Retention does not apply to any adjustment of the contract sum arising from the application of clauses 31(A) to (E). Application of clause 31(F), however, is to the unit rates of the work completed and as such, is subject to retention in the normal way.

Payments to sub-contractors

Under clause 27(c) of the conditions of contract the architect may request the contractor to furnish him with reasonable proof that amounts included in previous certificates in respect of nominated sub-contractors' work have been paid. It is good practice for this to be done as a matter of course before each certificate is issued, rather than periodically at the architect's discretion. Indeed where the warranty agreement is being used it must be done as one of the conditions of the warranty is that, in the event of the contractor failing to pay the sub-contractor the amount due under an interim certificate, the employer must pay the sub-contractor direct and deduct the amount so paid from the money due to the contractor.

Where the warranty agreement is not in use there is no obligation on the employer to make direct payments in this way, but he has discretion under the terms of the contract entitling him to do so.

It is not always easy to obtain satisfactory evidence that payments have in fact been made to nominated sub-contractors, partly because the payments are not in any case due to be made until shortly before the next certificate valuation is due and partly because receipts are no longer issued as a matter of course. The task of verifying these payments is usually undertaken by the quantity surveyor and he should make the necessary arrangements with the contractor at the start of the contract.

He can do this either by arranging that he receives the reply slips from the architect's notification to the nominated sub-contractors, or by asking the general contractor to produce receipts for such payments. If the latter method is chosen, and failure by sub-contractors to return the slips may make this necessary, the contractor should be told well in advance that receipts will be required. He can then make arrangements for receipts to be issued.

Retention

Clauses 30 (3) and (4) set out the contract arrangements for retention, the actual percentage to be retained and the limit of retention being inserted in the appendix to the conditions.

On the issue by the architect of the certificate of practical completion the contractor shall be entitled to receive a certificate releasing one moiety of the retention held.

It should be noted that clause 27 (e) provides machinery whereby the architect can release final payment to any nominated sub-contractor before final payment is due to the contractor. Two points are important in this sub-clause:

(a) The architect is under no contractual obligation to secure final payment to a nominated sub-contractor.

(b) If, however, the architect desires to secure final payment to a nominated sub-contractor, he must, as a condition precedent to issuing a certificate including such final payment, ensure that 'such sub-contractor has satisfactorily indemnified the contractor against latent defects'.

The second moiety of retention is released on the expiration of the defects liability period, or on the issue of the certificate of completion of making good defects provided there are no defects. This is normally before the issue of the final certificate.

Value Added Tax

Value Added Tax is under the control of Customs and Excise and is subject to the provisions of Finance Acts. The responsibility for the payment of this tax is that of the contractor; he in turn will invoice the employer appropriately. The employer will require advice from the architect and quantity surveyor at an early stage of a building scheme and they should be in a position to assist with this information. It is recommended that interim and final certificates issued by the architect should state that VAT is excluded and neither the architect nor the quantity surveyor should put themselves in a position of certifying the amount of tax that should be paid.

EXAMPLE 9

Quantity Surveyor.
of   .

Architect/S.O.   .
of   .

Employer   .
of   .

Contractor   .
of   .

Works   .
at   .

Valuation

No:

Date

QS Reference

I/We have made, under the terms of the Contract, an interim valuation as at

† and I/we report as follows:—

Gross valuation   [including nominated sub-contractors' values from
                         attached statement   *]   £

Less the value of any work or material notified to me/us by the Architect/S.O.
in writing, as not being in accordance with the Contract   £

                                                                              £

Less retention—either [% of £   *]   £

            —or   [from attached statement   *]   £

                                                                              £

Less previously CERTIFIED   £

Balance (in words)   £

Contract sum   £

Signature: Quantity Surveyor.

Notes:
  (i) All the above amounts are exclusive of V.A.T.
  (ii) The balance stated is subject to any statutory deductions which the Employer may be obliged to
       make under the provisions of the Finance (No. 2) Act 1975 where the Employer is classed as a
       "contractor" for the purposes of the Act.
  (iii) It is assumed that the Architect/S.O. will:—
       (a) satisfy himself that there is no further work or material which is not in accordance with
           the Contract.
       (b) unless otherwise agreed, notify Nominated sub-contractors of payments due to them.
       (c) satisfy himself, if he wishes, that previous payments to Nominated sub-contractors have been
           discharged.
  (iv) The Certificate of payment should be issued within seven days of the date indicated thus†.
  (v) Action by the Contractor should be taken only on the basis of figures contained in the Certificate
      of payment.

© 1977 RICS   * Delete as appropriate.   n.j.a.

EXAMPLE 9 *(cont.)*

Statement of Nominated sub-contractors Value

This Statement of Nominated sub-contractors Values relates to Valuation

No:

for Works .

at .

Date

.

QS Reference

.

Nominated sub-contractor	Total to date	Certified previously	Balance

n.j.a.

EXAMPLE 9 *(cont.)*

Statement of Retention

This Statement of Retention relates to Valuation

for Works .
at .

No:

Date

.

QS Reference

.

1. Retention percentage on Interim Certificates issued before Certificate of
    Practical Completion [Cl. 30(3)(a)]   % of
    [£   less deduction of £   *]   £   £

2. One-half retention percentage on Interim Certificates issued after
    Certificate of Practical Completion but before Certificate of Making   % of
    Good Defects [Cl. 30(3)(b)]
    [£   less deduction of £   *]   £   £ _____

3. Total amount of retention   £

4. Total of ALL previous releases   £

5. Releases included in this Valuation   .

5.1 Release of balance of retention to nominated sub-contractors [Cl. 27(e)]†   £

    Sub-contractor   £

    Sub-contractor   £

    Sub-contractor   £

5.2 Release of one-half retention percentage on the total value of any relevant
    part [Cl. 16(f)(i)] as stated in the Certificate issued on Partial
    Possession   £

5.3 Release of balance of retention percentage on the total value of any
    relevant part [Cl. 16(f)(ii)] as stated in the Certificate of Making Good
    Defects   £

5.4 Release of one-half of the amounts retained on issue of the Certificate of
    Practical Completion [Cl. 30(4)(b)]   £

5.5 Release of residue of amounts retained on issue of the Certificate of Making
    Good Defects [Cl. 30(4)(c)]   £
                                                                      _____ £
                                                                                          _____

    Retention   £
                                                                                          _____

* This deduction is the total of any amounts payable under Clauses 4(2), 11(6), 24, 31A to E, and 34.
† It is assumed that the Contractor has obtained satisfactory indemnity against latent defects and
  notified the Architect/S.O. accordingly.

n.j.a.

EXAMPLE 10

Architect's name
and address:

**Interim
certificate**

Serial No: 0014764

Employer's name
and address:

Issue date:
Valuation date:
Instalment No:
Job reference:

Contractor's name
and address:

① I/We certify that in accordance with
Clause 30 of the Standard Form of Building Contract, 1963 Edition,

under the Contract

dated: in the sum of £

for the Works:

situate at:

interim payment as detailed below is due from the Employer to the Contractor

Total value . . . . £
includes the value of works by nominated sub-contractors as detailed on
direction form no.   dated

Less retention . . . . £
after deducting any retentions released previously or herewith
(as detailed on the attached statement of retention ②)

Balance (cumulative total amount certified for payment) . . . . £

Less cumulative total amount previously certified for payment . . . . . . £

Amount due for payment on this certificate . . . . £

(in words)

All the above amounts are exclusive of VAT

Signed_____Architect

Contractor's provisional assessment of total of amounts included in above
certificate on which VAT will be chargeable   £ _____ at ____ %

This is not a Tax Invoice

Notes: (1) Where the form of contract is the Agreement for Minor Building Works 1968, delete this line and insert
'Clause 10 of the Agreement for Minor Building Works first issued 1968'.
(2) Delete words in parentheses if not applicable.
(3) This form may be used for the purposes of releasing retention on practical completion, on partial posssesion
or on making good defects. When used for this purpose and no statement of retention is issued, insert here
appropriate wording from the following:
'including release on practical completion/partial possession/making good defects'.

© RIBA Publications Ltd. 1977

52

EXAMPLE 10 *(cont.)*

Direction
of amounts included for
nominated sub-contractors
in interim certificate

Architect's name
and address:

to Contractor
of:

Issue date:
Valuation date:
Instalment No:
Job reference:

In accordance with Clause 27 of the Standard Form of Building Contract,
1963 Edition, I/we direct under the Contract dated:_____

for the Works:
situate at: _____

that the following amounts are included in the interim certificate
no._____dated_____and are therefore
due to be paid to the nominated sub-contractors listed below.

Nominated sub-contractor	All amounts are exclusive of VAT		
	Total to date	Certified previously	Balance included in certificate ①

The sums stated are the GROSS amounts due to the named nominated sub-contractor(s). No account has
been taken of any retentions which the Contractor might withhold under the terms of the sub-contract(s),
or of any discounts for cash to which the Contractor might be entitled if settling the accounts within 14 days.

② The Contractor is required to furnish proof of discharge of the above stated
amounts in accordance with Clause 27(c).

Signed_____Architect

Notes: ① Indicate where the sum includes final payment. Final payments should only be included if the Contractor
has confirmed receipt of satisfactory indemnity from the nominated sub-contractor.
② Delete if not applicable.

©RIBA Publications Ltd. 1976

53

EXAMPLE 11

To:
    (Architect)

CERTIFICATE No.
(Interim/Final)
 Job: ....
 Job No............ Date................

CONTRACTOR ....

CONTRACT SUM: £.............................

The value of work executed and materials delivered to site, including value of variations and work carrie
out by nominated sub-contractors up to (date).......................is as follows:

                      £

Work executed ..   ..

Materials on site ..   ..

Deduct retention   ..   ..

Add/Deduct on account of fluctuations in rates of wages and prices of
           materials ..   ..

Deduct amount previously certified ..   ..

                    NET AMOUNT DUE (including VAT) £

The above sums include gross payments to Nominated Sub-Contractors as listed overleaf. These paymen
are subject to retention and cash discount.

Date.................................   Signed..
                                            Quantity Surveyor

I/WE CERTIFY that the sum of £
(amount in writing) ....
is due to (Contractor) ....
and should be paid within 14 days in accordance with the terms of the Contract.
Payments are to be made to Nominated Sub-Contractors as listed overleaf.

Date.................................   Signed..
                                            Architect

EXAMPLE 11 *(cont.)*

GROSS AMOUNTS INCLUDED FOR NOMINATED SUB-CONTRACTORS
(Subject to retention and cash discount)

Name	Included in this certificate £	Previously included £	Total included to date £

EXAMPLE 12

Architect's name
and address

to nominated
sub-contractor

I/We inform you that under the terms of the Contract for the

works known as

situate at

a certificate has been issued for presentation to the employer

The contractor

of

has been directed that in the said certificate an amount is due to you as follows

Notification

to nominated sub-contractor
concerning amount included
in certificate

Serial no.

Date of issue

Date of valuation

Instalment no.

Gross total to date	Certified previously	Balance included in certificate
£	£	£

Signed

Architect/Supervising officer

The sum stated is the gross amount due. No account has been taken of any retentions which the contractor might withhold under the terms
of the sub-contract or of any discounts for cash to which the contractor might be entitled if settling the account within 14 days of the
receipt of the architect's certificate or of a duplicate copy thereof

EXAMPLE 13

DRAW & DRAW, F.F.R.I.B.A. Chartered Architects, 13 Corb's Buildings, London, SW1 3BS 01-930 0001	**NOTIFICATION TO SUB-CONTRACTOR** **OF ISSUE OF CERTIFICATE** Job .... Job No............ Date...................

To : ....
....
....
....
....

We have today issued to the General Contractor Certificate No............ which includes a sum
calculated to bring the total payment to you up to £ _____ less retention and cash
discount.

....
Architect

To : Measures & Partners,
Chartered Quantity Surveyors,
1 Dims Place,
London, SW1 5AB   Date................................

Job ....
Job No. ....

We have now received from the General Contractor all payments due to us in accordance with
Certificate No..............

....
Nominated Sub-contractor

Chapter 7

COMPLETION, DEFECTS AND THE FINAL ACCOUNT

It can be said that completion of a building contract falls under two main headings, namely:
1. Practical completion of the works
2. Completion of the contract.

Practical completion

Practical completion of the works is referred to in clause 15 of the conditions of contract and it is a date determined by the architect when he is required to issue a certificate clearly stating that the contract has reached this specific stage. In determining the date of practical completion of the works the architect should be completely satisfied with the answers to the following questions, as this date has an important influence on the contract and any legal dispute which might arise:

1. Has the work been carried out in accordance with the contract documents and architect's instructions?
2. Is the building in a suitable state to be taken over by the employer for its full and proper use?

With the issue of the certificate of practical completion the following take effect automatically in accordance with the conditions of contract:

1. The contractor becomes entitled to payment of one moiety of the total of the retention fund (clause 30 (4) (b)).
2. The defects liability period begins (clause 15).
3. The contractor is relieved of his obligations to insure the works in accordance with clause 20 (A).
4. The period of final measurement begins (clause 30).
5. Matters for arbitration dependent upon the issuing of the certificate of practical completion can be pursued.

Very often the architect finds that the building is ready for occupation although a number of minor items have not been completed by the contractor. In these circumstances the architect may be prepared to issue his certificate of practical completion but he would be well advised to specify in detail to the contractor those items incomplete. This may also apply to defective work which the architect requires to be remedied immediately and the architect's certificate should include the schedule of uncompleted work and defective items.

A copy of the RIBA Certificate of Practical Completion is shown in example 14.

Sectional completion

Sectional completion arises from a planned programme of the work and the completion dates for each section form part of the contract. These completion dates should be shown in the Appendix to the Sectional Completion Supplement to the contract and the allocation of the cost of each section will also have been determined at contract stage. The architect is required to issue a certificate of practical completion at the completion of each section and the certificate for the final section will be his certificate of practical completion for the whole contract. The contractor is entitled to one moiety of the retention fund allocated in direct ratio with the cost of the section completed. For each certificate of practical completion for a section the full operation of the contract (e.g. liquidated damages for non-completion, arbitration) takes effect for that particular section. If the contract is large it is quite feasible to have a situation arising when a certificate of practical completion is issued on one section when other sections have not started. In addition, final certificates can be issued on sections when other sections are not finished. The certificate to be issued by the architect in these circumstances is the same for practical completion (example 14, part a) suitably amended.

Partial possession

The difference between sectional completion and partial possession has been explained in chapter 2. Sectional completion arises from a planned programme of phased completion; partial possession results from partial completion and is an *ad hoc* situation covered by clause 16.

If the employer (in agreement with the contractor) takes possession of a part of the building at a time before practical completion of the whole of the works is reached, the architect is required, within seven days of possession being taken, to issue a certificate stating his approximate value of this part. The contractor is then entitled to one moiety of the retention fund in direct ratio of the architect's valuation of the part of the building occupied to the total value of the contract. Likewise the defects liability period commences for that part of the building at the date of the architect's certificate. This certificate for partial completion only applies to the release of one moiety of the retention fund and the commencement of the defects liability period in relation to the relevant part. It does not affect the period of final measurement, nor the procedures for arbitration which rely solely on the Certificate of Practical Completion for the whole of the works.

At the time of partial completion of any part of the building the value of insurance and amount of liquidated damages for non-completion must be reviewed in accordance with clauses 16(d) and 16(e) of the contract; here again the adjustment reduction is in direct ratio of the valuation of the building work handed over to the total value of the contract.

The certificate to be issued by the architect for partial completion is again the same for practical completion but in this case it is part b of example 14.

Occupation of the building

When practical completion is reached the employer takes over the building and the contractor ceases to be responsible for the site and relinquishes its possession to the owner. At this stage the architect and contractor should arrange a 'handing-over' meeting with the employer and ensure that he or his staff fully understands the operation of any equipment in the building such as heating plants, lifts, electric fuses and the like. In addition certain items of the building may require a special procedure for maintenance or repair and this information should be passed to the employer in a precise manner and should be confirmed in writing. Also as the possession of the site changes hands the responsibility for fire insurance, third-party liability and insurance generally must be taken over by the owner.

Within as short a time as possible after occupation of the building the architect should ensure that the contractor has removed all items of plant and surplus materials. All pipes, fuse boxes and the like should be properly marked or labelled and copies of drawings showing the building as constructed including services drawings should be given to the employer. One copy of these drawings should be deposited with a third party, say the bank of the employer, so that in the event of fire a full set of proper records of the building would be available for use in its repair or reconstruction. Good practice in this respect is covered by the RIBA maintenance manual.

Defects

During the defects liability period any defects, shrinkages or other faults which appear in the building and which are due to materials or workmanship not in accordance with the contract or due to frost occurring before practical completion of the contract, are to be specified by the architect in a schedule of defects. The method adopted in preparing this schedule is usually twofold. In the first place the architect should advise the employer to keep a proper record of all defects that appear from time to time. Some definite arrangement should be agreed so that any serious defect requiring immediate attention would be reported at once to the architect while items of a minor nature could be recorded in list form.

Secondly, at the completion of the defects liability period the architect in conjunction with the consultants responsible for the supervision of the work, should carry out detailed inspections of the building. From these inspections and from the information gained from the employer, the schedule of defects is prepared and clause 15 requires that it is delivered to the contractor within fourteen days after the expiration of the defects liability period.

The contractor has to rectify the items in the schedule of defects within a reasonable time and at his own expense. This equally applies to any item of defect which may occur during the defects liability period and which in the opinion of the architect should have immediate attention. If the contractor fails to remedy the defective items within a reasonable time the architect may instruct another contractor to do the work and deduct the charge of this second contractor from the total of the final account.

At the time these maintenance items are being cleared the architect may ask the contractor to carry out some minor additional work to the original contract. Such work is not part of the original contract, and should be charged entirely separately, probably on a daywork basis; it may, of course, be included in the final account under a suitable heading.

Completion

When the architect is satisfied that all defective work has been made good he must issue a certificate to that effect. The standard form for this purpose issued by the RIBA is shown in example 15. At the same time he should ensure that he has obtained all record drawings from specialist firms. He is then in a position to consider the completion of the contract. Completion is defined by the issue by the architect of the Certificate of Making Good Defects. Clause 30 requires that this certificate must be issued within three months of whichever of the following is the latest:

1. The end of the defects liability period, or
2. The completion of the making-good of defects, or
3. The receipt by the architect (or quantity surveyor) of the documents from contractor relating to the accounts of nominated sub-contractors and nominated suppliers.

Final account

In order that the architect can issue his final certificate he requires from the quantity surveyor the final account. The method of preparation of this document is set down in clause 11 of the conditions of contract and it is accepted that each surveyor may prepare his details in the manner best suited for each job. However, the adjustment of the contract sum, in the final account falls under the following headings:

1. Variations.
2. Remeasurement of provisional quantities in the bills of quantities.
3. Nominated sub-contractors' accounts.
4. Nominated suppliers' accounts.
5. Loss and expense caused by disturbance of regular progress of works (clause 24).
6. Fluctuations in rates of labour and prices of materials (clause 31) (if applicable).

The above items should be shown separately and clearly in the final account and the amount of each variation and the amount due to each nominated sub-contractor and nominated supplier should be given. In preparing the final account the surveyor must provide all reasonable facilities for the contractor to be present when measurements and details are taken or recorded. In this connection it is usual and advisable for the surveyor to agree with the contractor a suitable programme and procedure for measurement so that as the document is prepared it is agreed step by step.

The contract provides for a period of final measurement and the quantity surveyor is required to complete his final account and present it to the contractor within that period. However, the draft final account is a very effective implement in maintaining cost control of the contract if it is started as the building work begins and at monthly intervals is brought up-to-date as far as possible. From this draft account a report on known and anticipated expenditure can be prepared and submitted to the architect at, say, monthly intervals as a financial forecast of the probable final cost. This also enables the account to be finalised soon after the actual building work is complete and ensures that the interim payments to the contractor are realistic in relation to the value of the work carried out.

Much could be written on the detailed work required in the preparation of final accounts but in this book we are more concerned with the procedure. Safe to say, however, that delays in settlement of the final account are a cost to the contractor, and in most cases the employer also is keen to know his ultimate financial commitment. The architect, surveyor, and consultants should always remember that they have a contractual duty to adhere to the date set down in the contract for completion of the account and the contractor should give every assistance in the prompt accounting for sub-contractors' and suppliers' accounts, agreement of measurements and prices and similar matters.

It is important that the measurement and financial assessment of variations should be completed as speedily as possible. Clause 11 (5) requires that the financial adjustment of the contract sum in respect of variations should be taken into account when preparing interim certificates. The provisions of this clause should be observed as it is bad practice for the contractor to have levied against him a hidden retention in respect of extra work ordered through variations for which no financial allowance is made until the final account is completed.

Final certificate

Once the final account has been prepared by the surveyor, and the architect is satisfied on all other points previously referred to he can issue his final certificate. This will normally be on the standard form shown in example 16. This certificate releases to the contractor the second moiety of the retention fund if not previously released. Hence the amount of the final certificate is the gross amount of the final account less the amount of all previous payments.

Under clause 22, if the architect considers that the contractor should have completed within the time fixed under the contract and has failed to do so, then he shall certify in writing to this effect. In that case the employer is entitled to deduct the liquidated damages shown in the appendix to the contract.

Final Account

EXAMPLE 14

Architect's name
and address:

Job title and no :

RIBA Certificate of

Practical
Completion

or Partial Completion

o [main contractor]

Serial no.:

In accordance with the Standard Form of Building Contract, I we certify that subject to the completion of any outstanding items, and/or making good of any defects, shrinkages and other faults which appear during the defects liability period,

[delete a or b as necessary]

a   the Works were in my our opinion practically completed as described in Clause 15(1) on:

and that the said defects liability period will end on:

b a part of the Works, namely:

the approximate value of which I estimate for the purposes of Clause 16 (but for no other)
to be: £

was taken into possession under Clause 16 on:

and that in relation to the said part of the Works, the said defects liability period will for the
purpose specified in Clause 16(b) end on

I/we declare that a certificate for one moiety of the retention moneys deducted under previous certificates in respect of the said Works or part thereof is to be issued in accordance with the Conditions of Contract.

Signature: Architect / Supervising Officer   Date:

Original to: ☐   Copies to: Employer ☐   Quantity surveyor ☐   Clerk of works ☐   Architect's file ☐
Contractor

Structural consultant ☐   Heating consultant ☐   Electrical consultant ☐   ☐

c RIBA 1971

63

EXAMPLE 15

EXAMPLE 15

Architect's name
and address :

RIBA Certificate of

Making Good Defects

Job title and no :

To [main contractor] :

Serial no. :

In accordance with the Standard Form of Building Contract, I/we certify that all outstanding items and all defects, shrinkages and other faults which appeared during the defects liability period in respect of:

[delete a or b as necessary]

a   the Works were in my/our opinion completed and/or made good in accordance with
Clause 15(4) on:

b   the part of the Works referred to in my/our Certificate of Partial Completion dated:

were in my/our opinion completed and/or made good in accordance with Clause 16(c) on:

I/we declare that a certificate for the residue of the retention moneys deducted under previous certificates in respect of the said Works or part thereof is to be issued in accordance with the Conditions of Contract.

Signature :   Architect / Supervising Officer   Date:

Original to:
Contractor ☐   Copies to: Employer ☐   Quantity surveyor ☐   Clerk of works ☐   Architect's file ☐

Structural consultant ☐   Heating consultant ☐   Electrical consultant ☐   ☐

© RIBA 1971

64

EXAMPLE 16

Architect's name
and address:

**Final
certificate**

Employer's name
and address:

Serial No:
Issue date:
Job reference:

Contractor's name
and address:

In accordance with Clause 30(6) of the Standard Form of Building Contract,
1963 Edition, I/We certify under the Contract

dated: _____

for the Works: _____

situate at: _____

that   1. The Contract Sum adjusted as necessary in accordance with the terms of
the above-mentioned Conditions is . . . . £

and   2. ① The sum of the amount paid to the Contractor under Interim Certificates
and of any payments not included in that amount made in respect of the
amount named as the Limit of Retention Fund is/The sum of the amounts
already paid to the Contractor under Interim Certificates and Certificates
issued under sub-clause (4) (b) and (4) (c) of the above-mentioned
condition is . . . . £

and that . . . . £

(in words) _____

is a balance due from/to ② the Employer to/from ② the Contractor and
subject to any deductions authorised by the Contract Conditions shall be a
debt payable from the fourteenth day after the presentation/issue ③ of this
certificate.

All the above amounts are exclusive of VAT

Signed_____Architect

Notes: ① Delete as appropriate. In paragraph 2 above the second alternative should be used where the amendment
issued in January 1972 and incorporated in the July 1972 revision of the contract applies.

② Delete as appropriate.

③ The word 'presentation' must be deleted if the certificate is issued under the Local Authorities Edition of the
Standard Form of Building Contract. Where the certificate is issued under the Private Edition the word
'presentation' must be deleted where a balance is due to the Employer; in other cases the word 'issue' must
be deleted.

c RIBA Publications Ltd. 1974

Chapter 8

DELAYS AND DISPUTES

Delay in the completion of the work is one of the most common causes of trouble encountered during the administration of building contracts. It is also one of the most justifiable causes of criticism of the building industry.

Broadly speaking delays can be considered under three headings:
1.	Delay caused by the contractor.
2.	Delay caused by the employer or his architect.
3.	Delay due to causes outside the control of the parties to the contract or their representatives.

The procedure to be followed when a delay occurs differs according to the causes of the delay in question, and the matter must therefore be considered separately under each of the foregoing.

Delays caused by the contractor

Coming within this heading are all those delays which can be avoided if the contractor proceeds efficiently and diligently with the running of the contract and the work itself. Under the terms of the contract the contractor is expected to take all possible steps to ensure that he has an adequate labour force on the job, that he has the specified materials on the job when they are needed and that the work is not held up by a delay on the part of nominated sub-contractors and nominated suppliers.

If the contractor does not take all possible steps to avoid such delays, there is no provision in the contract for the granting of an extension of time on account of them. The responsibility for them is the contractor's and when they occur the contractor may render himself liable to compensate the employer by the payment of liquidated damages under clause 22 of the conditions of contract.

Delays caused by nominated sub-contractors and suppliers when they occur are also a source of trouble. This is partly because it is frequently difficult to establish exactly who is responsible for such delays and partly because, where they are shown to be the sub-contractor's fault and where the contractor has done all he can to prevent them, the contractor is entitled under the conditions of contract to be granted an extension of time. The employer is deprived of his means of redress by way of liquidated damages.

The Form of Agreement between Employer and Nominated Sub-contractor establishes a direct relationship between the employer and the nominated sub-contractor and one of its conditions is that, if the sub-contractor is responsible for delaying the contract, the employer will have an enforceable remedy against the sub-contractor, despite the general contractor's right to an extension of time under clause 23 (g).

Finally if delays caused by the contractor are of a serious nature and if the contractor fails to take reasonable steps to rectify them, then the employer is empowered under clause 25 to determine the contract.

Delays caused by the employer or his architect

Causes of delay of this nature are provided for in clause 23 of the conditions of contract and may be summarised as follows:

(a) The issue of architect's instructions where there is a discrepancy in or divergence between the contract drawings and/or the contract bills, of which the contractor has given written notice.
(b) The issue of architect's instructions requiring a variation.
(c) The issue of architect's instructions with regard to the postponement of any of the work.
(d) The failure of the architect to issue to the contractor in due time necessary instructions, drawings, details or levels, for which the contractor has specifically applied in writing, provided such application was made at an appropriate time in relation to the work.
(e) Delay on the part of artists, tradesmen or others engaged by the employer to carry out work which is not part of the contract.
(f) Delay caused by the architect requiring completed work to be opened up or materials tested, provided such work or materials are found to be in accordance with the contract.

When delays of this nature occur, or as soon as it becomes apparent that they will occur, the contractor should notify the architect of a delay and if the architect is satisfied that the application is justified, the completion date for the work must be extended by an appropriate period in accordance with the conditions of contract.

Furthermore, if delays from these causes involve the contractor in direct loss or expense for which he would not otherwise be reimbursed, he will be entitled to recover such loss and expense under the provisions of clauses 11 (6) and 24.

In the event of delays of this nature continuing the contractor may, under clause 26, determine the contract. In such a case, however, the delay must have continued for a stated period, which should be inserted in the appendix to the contract. The period normally inserted for this is one month.

Delays due to causes outside the control of the parties to the contract

Clearly there are occasions when delays arise due to circumstances over which neither party to the contract, nor their respective representatives, have any control. Such delays are anticipated by clause 23 of the conditions of contract and may be summarised as follows:

(a) *Force majeure.*
(b) Exceptionally inclement weather.
(c) Loss or damage due to fire, lightning, explosion, storm, tempest, flood bursting or overflowing of water tanks or apparatus or pipes, earthquake, aircraft and other aerial devices or articles dropped therefrom, riot and civil commotion.
(d) Civil commotion, local combination of workmen, strike or lockout affecting any of the trades employed upon the works or any of the trades engaged in

the preparation, manufacture or transportation of any goods or materials required for the works.

(e) Delay on the part of nominated sub-contractors or nominated suppliers which the contractor has taken all practicable steps to avoid or reduce.

(f) Inability of the contractor for reasons beyond his control and which he could not reasonably have foreseen at the date of the contract to secure such labour, goods or materials as are essential for properly carrying out the work. (The printed conditions of contract provide for this clause to be deleted in whole or in part if not required. The architect and quantity surveyor should have given advice on this at the pre-contract stage.)

In the case of delays from such causes the contract provides in clause 23 for an extension of time to be granted in a similar manner as that set out above for delays caused by the employer or his architect. In such cases, however, there is no provision in the contract for the contractor to be reimbursed financially for any loss or additional expense which such delays may have caused him, it being contended that the burden of such delays shall be shared by the parties to the contract.

The interpretation of certain of these clauses may give rise to some dispute and it is perhaps advisable to look at some of them more closely.

The term *'force majeure'* is a somewhat ill-defined legal phrase. In its broadest usage it would appear to include acts of God, war, strikes, epidemics and any direct legislative or administrative interference. Several of these matters, however, are provided for separately in the building contract and it may therefore be said in this context to cover matters of a similar nature which are not specifically dealt with elsewhere.

The term 'exceptionally inclement weather' is frequently a source of argument in connection with delays in building work. The word 'exceptionally' is clearly the important one in this phrase and it must be considered according to the time of year and the conditions envisaged in the contract documents. Thus, if it were known at the time that a contract was let that the work was to be carried out during the winter months, and if that work is delayed by a fortnight of snow and frost during January, such a delay could not be regarded as due to exceptionally inclement weather. If, however, such work was held up by a continuous period of snow and frost, from early January until the end of March, an extension of time would clearly be justified under this clause. It is also important to consider the location of the work, as what may be regarded as exceptionally inclement weather in the south of England would not necessarily be regarded as the same in the Shetland Isles. In this respect local weather records can prove a valuable guide to the normal weather conditions one can expect to encounter in a particular area. In certain circumstances such delays may be avoided by providing in the contract for additional protection and even temporary heating arrangements.

In the case of delays by nominated sub-contractors and nominated suppliers, and delays due to the contractor being unable to obtain labour or materials at the right time, the contract conditions impose a forceful obligation on the contractor to take every possible step to avoid such delays occurring. Should they occur, the architect has a clear obligation to satisfy himself that the contractor has taken such steps before an extension of time is justified.

Clearly it is in everybody's interest that all possible steps to avoid delay should be taken and when the architect's responsibilities in this connection are considered two particular points should be borne in mind. As stated above, if the delay is caused by the employer or the architect the contractor is entitled to seek an extension of time and also to be reimbursed for any loss he may incur as a result of the delay. In addition to this, the delay might involve a breach of the contract by the employer for which the contractor may have a right to claim damages at Common Law. Such a situation is foreseen by the conditions of contract and clause 24 (2) makes it clear that a contractor's right in this connection is preserved, notwithstanding any extension of time or reimbursement for loss or expense which he may have been granted. Thus delays caused by the architect, who is not a party to the contract, may involve the employer in considerable loss and expense and he may well be justified in seeking redress against the architect.

In the event of delays occurring or being foreseen it is most important that the contractor should notify the architect without delay. This will enable the architect to take any steps that are within his power to avoid or reduce the delay, if that is possible, and will at the same time ensure that the contractor is granted an extension of time if one is justified. Prompt action in dealing with delays also helps to avoid serious disputes arising during the later stages of the work. For this reason it is in practice advisable for the architect not to await notice in writing from the contractor but, if he foresees delays occurring, to take the matter up with the contractor on his own initiative immediately. One of the benefits of dealing with delays as soon as possible is to re-establish the programme so that everybody is aware of the new target that has been set for completion and can re-schedule their work accordingly.

Damages and bonuses

Clause 22 of the conditions of contract states that if the contractor fails to complete the works by the date of completion or by any extended date if an extension of time has been granted, and if the architect certifies that the work should have been completed by that date, then the contractor shall pay or allow to the employer the sum calculated at the rate stated in the appendix to the conditions of contract as liquidated and ascertained damages. The amount of the damages is usually stated as a given sum per day or per week. It is important that this sum should be carefully and realistically calculated at the time the tender documents are being prepared. The amount should be a proper estimate of the damage the employer is likely to suffer if the work is not completed on time. It is not intended as a penalty and should an unrealistically high figure be included the Court may well set aside the amount stated in the contract in favour of a realistic assessment of the damages actually suffered. The Court, however, will not normally interfere if the amount stated is a genuine estimate of the damages.

It is frequently argued that there is little point in putting an amount for liquidated and ascertained damages in the appendix to the contract, as the provisions of clause 22 are very seldom enforceable. There is no justification for this argument, however, provided the specific and implied terms of the contract are adhered to, particularly those in clause 23 regarding extension of time, which have already been discussed in this chapter.

It is also sometimes argued that it is easier to enforce the liquidated damages clause if a bonus clause is inserted in the contract. This, however, is erroneous and appears to arise from confusion between liquidated damages and a penalty. As stated above the damages are intended to be a genuine estimate of damages and not a penalty. If a penalty clause as such is to be inserted in the contract, it should be kept quite separate from liquidated and ascertained damages, and certainly a bonus clause should accompany it. In such a case a given sum will be stated as being payable by the contractor to the employer in the event of delay in completion of the work or payable by the employer to the contractor in the event of early completion. Alternatively a bonus clause only can be inserted under which the contractor will receive a certain sum if he completes by an agreed date, this sum being reduced in stages if the contractor does not complete on time until a further agreed date is reached when the bonus ceases to apply at all.

There must be a clear agreement by both parties to the contract beforehand as to what is a reasonable length of time for carrying out the work, and it is in the interests of both parties that the amount of such penalty or bonus should be a sensible figure in relation to the value of the work. As some negotiation and agreement on these specific matters is advisable, it is probably better not to include bonus and penalty clauses in the contract documents, but to negotiate them later with the successful contractor and make them the subject of a separate agreement.

Disputes and arbitration

Many disputes arise in the course of building operations, but most of these are of a minor nature and are settled fairly and amicably by those concerned. From time to time, however, matters come into dispute which cannot be easily settled and subsequently become the subjects of claims by one party to the contract against the other. It is not feasible to consider in detail what matters might give rise to disputes and how they should be dealt with, as each case must be considered on its merits. In general, it can be said that most disputes and claims can be traced back to failure by one of the parties to the contract, one of the professional advisers or some other party connected with the contract to do his work efficiently, to express himself clearly or to understand the full implications of instructions issued to or received by him.

In 1963 the National Joint Consultative Committee of Architects, Quantity Surveyors and Builders published a booklet entitled *Building Project Management* and paragraph fourteen of this booklet contains a pertinent comment on this subject: 'None of the parties can regard the making of claims (or the infliction of penalties) as reflecting credit on their management. The more thorough the planning of the work and the more efficient the management of the contract, the less will claims and penalties occur.'

In the event of a serious dispute arising every effort should be made to reach a fair settlement by negotiation. If, however, this proves impossible the dispute should be referred to arbitration in accordance with clause 35 of the conditions of contract. The procedure for doing this is quite straightforward.

In the first instance the party to the contract wishing to refer the matter to arbitration must ask the other party, in writing, to concur in the appointment of an arbitrator. This appointment may be made by an agreement between the parties, or, if they cannot agree on a suitable person, the appointment will be made by the president or a vice-president of the RIBA. The contract itself contains an agreement that matters in duspute shall be submitted to arbitration, and this written request for the appointment of an arbitrator automatically refers the matter in dispute to him when appointed.

There are four matters of dispute which may be dealt with by arbitration during the progress of the work. These are:
1. A dispute arising in connection with the appointment of a new architect or quantity surveyor in accordance with the articles of agreement.

2. A dispute as to whether an architect's instruction is valid.
3. A dispute as to whether a certificate has been improperly withheld or has not been properly prepared in accordance with the conditions of contract.
4. A dispute arising in connection with an outbreak of hostilities or war damage.

Arbitration on all other matters shall not be commenced until after the practical completion of the works or the determination of the contract, unless with the written consent of both parties to the contract. Any matter of dispute in connection with a contract may be referred to arbitration including such matters as are in the ordinary way solely in the discretion of the architect.

" ... delay on the part of artists ... "

Chapter 9

BANKRUPTCY

This chapter deals with bankruptcy in the case of building contracts.

In certain respects the effects of liquidation or winding-up of a company are different from the effect of bankruptcy. For example, although by virtue of section 317 of the Companies Act 1948 the bankruptcy rules are applied in the winding up of insolvent English companies, the law as to 'reputed ownership' which is touched upon below may not be applicable in winding-up. To avoid excessive duplication and repetition, what follows is confined to bankruptcy and it is thought that its method of approach to problems created by bankruptcy may prove helpful with reference also to liquidation and winding-up.

Whereas in all the other chapters the practice described either happens fairly frequently or else is entirely within our control so that it can be made to happen, the procedure concerning bankruptcy can only occur when this event takes place. Fortunately it does not very often occur with the contractor and there are very few instances indeed of it occurring with the employer. As the procedure for bankruptcy of the contractor is of course entirely different from that of the employer, this chapter will first deal with the procedure in the case of the contractor's bankruptcy. Afterwards, but much more briefly, because the case is simpler, the procedure in the bankruptcy of the employer will be dealt with.

As bankruptcy of one of the parties to a contract under the JCT conditions is relatively infrequent, little is known about the practice and procedure to be adopted. In addition bankruptcy matters rarely find their way into the courts and there is little case law to refer to.

Contract provisions

As the understanding of the procedure is so closely tied to the clauses in the contract, the relevant clauses are quoted here in full.

They are clauses 25 (2) and (3):

(2) In the event of the Contractor becoming bankrupt or making a composition or arrangement with his creditors or having a winding-up order made or (except for purposes of reconstruction) a resolution for voluntary winding-up passed or a provisional liquidator, receiver or manager of his business or undertaking duly appointed, or possession taken, by or on behalf of the holders of any debentures secured by a floating charge, of any property comprised in or subject to the floating charge, the employment of the Contractor under this contract shall be forthwith automatically determined but the said employment may be reinstated and continued if the Employer and the Contractor his trustee in bankruptcy liquidator receiver or manager as the case may be shall so agree.

(3) In the event of the employment of the Contractor being determined as aforesaid and so long as it has not been reinstated and continued, the following shall be the respective rights and duties of the Employer and Contractor:

BANKRUPTCY

(a) The Employer may employ and pay other persons to carry out and complete the Works and he or they may enter upon the Works and use all temporary buildings, plant, tools, equipment, goods and materials intended for, delivered to and placed on or adjacent to the Works, and may purchase all materials and goods necessary for the carrying out and completion of the Works.

(b) The Contractor shall, if so required by the Employer or Architect within fourteen days of the date of determination assign to the Employer without payment the benefit of any agreement for the supply of materials or goods and/or for the execution of any work for the purposes of this Contract but on the terms that a supplier or sub-contractor shall be entited to make any reasonable objection to any further assignment thereof by the Employer. In any case the Employer may pay any supplier or sub-contractor for any materials or goods delivered or works executed for the purposes of this contract (whether before or after the date of determination) in so far as the price thereof has not already been paid by the Contractor. The Employer's rights under this paragraph are in addition to his rights to pay nominated sub-contractors as provided in Clause 27 (c) of these conditions and payments made under this paragraph may be deducted from any sum due or to become due to the Contractor.

(c) The Contractor shall as and when required in writing by the Architect so to do (but not before) remove from the Works and temporary buildings, plant, tools, equipment, goods and materials belonging to or hired by him. If within a reasonable time after any such requirement has been made the Contractor has not complied therewith, then the Employer may (but without being responsible for any loss or damage) remove and sell any such property of the Contractor, holding the proceeds less all costs incurred to the credit of the Contractor.

(d) The Contractor shall allow or pay to the Employer in the manner hereinafter appearing the amount of any direct loss and/or damage caused to the Employer by the determination. Until after completion of the Works under paragraph (a) of this sub-clause the Employer shall not be bound by any provision of this contract to make any further payment to the Contractor, but upon such completion and the verification within a reasonable time of the accounts therefor the Architect shall certify the amount of expenses properly incurred by the Employer and the amount of any direct loss and/or damage caused to the Employer by the determination and, if such amounts when added to the monies paid to the Contractor before the date of determination exceed the total amount which would have been payable on due completion in accordance with this Contract, the difference shall be a debt payable to the Employer by the Contractor; and if the said amounts when added to the said monies be less than the said total amount, the difference shall be a debt payable by the Employer to the Contractor.

Law

The statute law mainly applicable is The Bankruptcy Act 1914 and the Companies Act 1948.

There is not as much case law available (especially recently) as might be expected but the following are some of the relevant cases, reference to which will be helpful to anyone involved in the bankruptcy of one of the parties to a building contract.

1. Re Harrison *ex parte* Jay (1880) 14 Ch.D. 19.
2. Re Walker *ex parte* Gould (1884) 13 Q.B.D. 454.

3. Re Asphaltic Wood Pavement Co., *ex parte* Lee & Chapman (1885) 30 Ch.D. 216; 54 L.J.Ch. 460; 53 L.T. 63; 33 W.R. 513.
4. Drew & Josolyne (1887) 18 Q.B.D. 590; 56 L.J.Q.B. 490; 57 L.J. 5; 35 W.R. 570.
5. Re Holt *ex parte* Gray (1888) 58 L.J.Q.B. 5.
6. Re Keen & Keen *ex parte* Collins (1902) 1 K.B. 555; 71 L.J.K.B. 487; 86 L.T. 235; 50 W.R. 334; 9 Manson 145.
7. Re Wilkinson *ex parte* Fowler (1905) 2 K.B. 713; 74 L.J.K.B. 969; 54 W.R. 157.
8. Heyman v Darwins (1942) A.C. 356.
9. Re Fox *ex parte* Oundle & Thrapston R.D.C. v The Trustee (1948) Ch. 407; 1948 L.J.R. 1733; 112 J.P. 294; 92 S.J. 310; 1948 1 All E.R. 849; 46 L.G.R. 305.
10. Re Tout & Finch (1954) 1 W.L.R. 178; 98 S.J. 62; (1954) 1 All E.R. 127; 52 L.G.R. 70.
11. Dunlop & Ranken Ltd v Hendall Steel Structures Ltd (1957) 3 All E.R. 344.
12. London Borough of Hounslow v Twickenham Garden Developments (1970) 3 All E.R. 326.
13. British Eagle v Air France (1975) 1 W.L.R. 758.

Procedure during contract

It is most important that the architect and quantity surveyor receiving intimation that the contractor is in financial difficulties should keep the matter strictly confidential. Apart from the possibility of libel or slander actions, the spread of this information could quickly drive him into more serious difficulties or bankruptcy, which he might otherwise have been able to avoid.

If the proper procedure permitted under the contract is carried out it will mitigate the difficulties arising on bankruptcy. One matter which the quantity suveyor should always check is that the contractor has paid the nominated sub-contractors amounts included for them in the previous certificate. If the contractor has not paid these, then the quantity surveyor will inform the architect who *shall*, in accordance with clause 27 (c), issue a certificate to that effect, whereupon the employer *may* pay such amounts himself and deduct the same from any sums due to the contractor.

In these circumstances it is more important than ever that certificate valuations are prepared as accurately as possible and should include the full value of all sub-contractor's work that has actually been done whether or not payment has been applied for.

Additional vigilance by the architect is required, and it is essential that he should let the quantity surveyor know of all work which has not been properly carried out, so that such work can be excluded from certificate valuations. In addition the clerk of works should ensure that no materials leave the site after having been delivered, except with the consent of the architect, who will check with the quantity surveyors whether or not they have been included in certificates. The quantity surveyor as mentioned earlier should be particularly accurate in his certificates in these circumstances and should be careful to resist any tendency to undervalue for safety which may lead to a bankruptcy which is nearly always disastrous from the employer's point of view.

Immediate procedure

As soon as the bankruptcy takes place the employment of the contractor under the contract is forthwith automatically determined. It is important to note the exact choice of these words. There is no need for any letters determining the employment of the contractor, and this is abundantly clear by the use of the words 'forthwith automatically' in the contract. It is also important to note that it is only the employment of the contractor which is determined not the contract itself. The contract goes on and the employer has various rights under it.

It is desirable that as soon as the bankruptcy becomes known, the site should be closed and no materials or plant allowed to leave it. The law regarding the vesting of materials in the event of bankruptcy is complex. The fact that the employer has bought the materials may not prevent them vesting in the trustees in bankruptcy if the 'reputed' or apparent ownership is in the contractor. Such 'reputed' ownership is more likely to result where materials are in the contractor's yard but it could in certain circumstances attach even to materials on the building site. The matter is dealt with in the Re Fox, *ex parte* Oundle and Thrapston R.D.C. case referred to above. The provisions in the standard contract dealing with unfixed goods and materials may not of themselves be sufficient to override the application of this principle of 'reputed ownership'.

As a matter of practice it is safest to assume that all materials on the site are in the ownership of the employer and to allow no one on the site under any pretext whatsoever. It is then up to the trustee in bankruptcy, or to a sub-contractor or supplier to prove that any particular materials are not vested in the employer.

If a clerk of works is employed he may be able to act as watchman during the day. But it will be prudent for the employer to engage a watchman whenever the clerk of works is not on the site. The danger of losing materials from a building site is always high, but is much higher in these particular circumstances. Further, those in charge of the site will have to deal with suppliers and sub-contractors who may wish to retrieve their own materials not fixed on the job.

The quantity surveyor will almost certainly, in any subsequent work for completing the job, require a list of unfixed materials on site. It is therefore a good idea for him to make this list as soon as possible. He and the architect should try to make immediate arrangements with the employer for getting all loose materials which are valuable and can be moved, under lock and key. It may well be that some, or all of this type of material is already locked up, in which case the keys should be obtained from the bankrupt contractor.

If the bankrupt contractor leaves some plant on the site which he had on hire, the employer may under the contract within fourteen days have the benefit of any plant agreement assigned to him. In this case the employer may pay for the plant hire and this expense will rank as one of the expenses to be taken into account under clause 25 (3) (d). As it would be exceedingly difficult to start the completion contract within fourteen days, it will often be better to require all plant which is on hire to be removed from the site without further payment. There are, however, obvious exceptions to this in the way of pumps and props which might have disastrous effects on the works if prematurely removed.

Concerning the contractor's own plant there will be no need to make any immediate cash payment to the trustee for this. It would be assumed that if the plant is required and the completion contractor realises it is available on the site that his price will be lower accordingly to the ultimate benefit of the trustee. Plant not required, however, should be released as soon as possible. Further it should be realised that the bankrupt contractor's plant may not be suitable for the completion contractor's organisation. It may therefore be more economical to release plant even though the same category of plant will still be required to complete.

Completion of contract

It will be necessary to arrange a meeting between all concerned to consider the best way of completing the contract. The employer, his professional advisers and all consultants should be at this meeting. There is no need to ask the trustee in bankruptcy to the meeting, in any case the creditors may not have appointed him yet. When he is appointed, however, he should be kept informed of the decisions that have been made. Likewise if a bond is coupled with the contract then the bond holder should be kept informed.

The trustee in bankruptcy himself may disclaim the contract which he is entitled statutorily to do. If required to decide whether he will disclaim or not the trustee must give notice of disclaimer within twenty-eight days or he will be deemed to have adopted the contract. Alternatively under the conditions of contract he may ask the employer if the contractor may be reinstated to complete the contract but it is up to the employer to say whether he agrees to this course or not. The third and perhaps the most usual course is for the employer to complete the contract.

The procedure to be adopted for the completion of the contract in the last mentioned case will depend on the extent of the work to be completed. If the contract has only just started, then it would be reasonable to go out to tender again asking the same type of contractor to tender for the completion of the work as in the original tender list. In this case the quantity surveyor could deal with the tendering documents by preparing a short bill of the work already carried out which would be an omission bill and that coupled with the original bill would form a bill of quantities of the work to be completed.

If the work is well in hand but far from complete, it may be best to get competitive tenders for completing, though sometimes it may be advantageous to negotiate with a single contractor a suitable contract for completion. The bond holder and the trustee in bankruptcy have no powers to refuse consent, but the employer might be in difficulties in later dealings with them if he has failed to convince them that he has taken due care to complete the work in a reasonably economical way. It would be as well if the employer could show that negotiating a contract was more economical than going to competitive tender again. Provided the negotiations are reasonable this may not be too difficult to show if time has been saved thereby.

The quantity surveyor will have to use his own judgment in these circumstances, whether it is quicker for him to produce a new document for the completion of the work, or whether it is still better to use the existing bills with an omission bill for work which has already been carried out.

If the work is substantially complete, what remains to be done may very often be in the nature of jobbing work. In these circumstances a completely different type of builder may be the best one to complete. Furthermore it may be better to complete on a prime cost contract having a fixed fee. It will be up to the quantity surveyor to weigh up the job with particular reference to the sub-contractors' work still to be done, and to make recommendations on the most suitable contract procedure for completion. If the client has a direct labour force it may be convenient for him to complete it in this manner, especially when one bears in mind that the existing sub-contractors may well be available to carry on.

One item that will be essential in the bills for completion will be a provisional sum to cover making good of defects left by the bankrupt contractor. Where these are actually known they can of course be measured, but it is necessary to make sure that this is covered as there will probably be some defects which do not make themselves apparent until the new contractor is on the site.

Most of the work in getting out the new contract documents will necessarily fall on the quantity surveyor; it will probably not be necessary for the architect to do other than re-issue his existing drawings as it will be obvious to the new contractor that he is only to execute that work which has not already been done. For the purpose of establishing a price, however, the quantity surveyor will have to prepare documents in one of the ways mentioned above and it is essential that he do this as quickly as possible.

Sub-contractors

It is generally thought that there is a distinct difference between the position of nominated sub-contractors under clause 27 of the conditions of contract and the contractor's own sub-contractors in the event of the main contractor's bankruptcy. However this difference may well be exaggerated. In each case there is a 'discretion' to make a payment direct to a sub-contractor who has executed work and has not been paid. This 'discretion' is spelt out in the case of the nominated sub-contractors in clause 27 (e), but the employer is quite free to do the same to other unpaid sub-contractors. It is thought, however, that this is rarely done in the case of the contractor's own sub-contractors, and it is not a course of action which the Group would advocate without taking advice in the light of particular circumstances. If in the case of payment to a nominated sub-contractor the main contractor's trustee in bankruptcy endeavoured to recover the amount of the payment from the employer, he would be met by the defence that the money has been paid direct to the sub-contractor as the employer's contract with the main contractor had entitled him to do. In the case of payment to one of the main contractor's own sub-contractors this defence would not be open to the employer, but as the sum recovered by the trustee would (it is thought) be held on trust for the sub-contractor the practical consequence of the distinction may be unimportant.

If the employer has paid direct to the sub-contractor (whether nominated under clause 27 or not) a sum *not* comprised in any payment made to the main contractor then he has not suffered any loss and has no claim against the main contractor or his trustee. If the employer has paid direct to the sub-contractor an amount which he has already paid to the main contractor, which the latter has failed to transmit, then his claim to recover the sum from the trustee must probably take its place with the claims of other creditors for the dividend out of the bankrupt's estate. The fact that he exercised a discretion to pay a sub-contractor direct (whether spelt out in the main contract or not) does not necessarily give him priority because his debt to the main contractor is not discharged by a direct payment to the sub-contractor.

The case of Tout & Finch appears to be distinguishable from the hypothesis last referred to. In Tout & Finch what gave priority to the sub-contractors over other creditors of the bankrupt was the contractual entitlement of a third party to make payment direct to the sub-contractor. However the case of Tout & Finch may have been overturned recently with the decision in *British Eagle* v *Air France* where it appears that it may not be possible to contract out of the general law regarding bankruptcy. Whenever direct payment is made to a sub-contractor after bankruptcy it is always advisable to get an indemnity from the sub-contractor in the eventuality of the payment being challenged.

The use of the form of warranty would not appear materially to affect the situation arising on the bankruptcy of the main contractor. The warranty does, however, safeguard the employer as far as the direct payments which he undertakes to make to nominated sub-contractors are concerned. The warranty provides that in the case of the main contractor's liquidation such direct payments need not be made if, by making them, the retention monies were to be reduced below the amount reasonably necessary to cover various payments which would have to be met in any case, including those for making good defects, meeting direct loss and/or damage recoverable under clause 25 of the main contract and paying other nominated sub-contractors under clause 27 (c).

There will very likely be a considerable number of sub-contractors to deal with and they will fall into two groups:

(a) those who have partially completed their work and
(b) those who have not yet started.

As sub-contracts should be drawn up in terms similar to the main contract there should be no difficulty for those who have not started. They will be invited to enter into a similar sub-contract with the new contractor when the new contract is placed.

Where sub-contractors have partially executed their work, it will probably be best for the quantity surveyor to negotiate with each in turn a price for completing. The quantity surveyor must take care, however, only to measure and assess the value of the work to be completed and not take any account of the fact that the sub-contractor may not have been paid for all the work he has already done. There will normally, in the absence of collateral undertakings of wider scope than the warranty previously referred to, be no obligation on the employer to pay this amount; it will be entirely at his discretion. If the employer is a public authority it may well be that it will decide that public funds should not be used in this way if it means that the nominated sub-contractor will be paid in full but that the employer will only be reimbursed a small fraction in the pound.

The quantity surveyor in negotiating for the completion of the sub-contract should bear these things in mind because it may well be that the sub-contractor will not agree to complete unless he is paid in full for the work done before the bankruptcy occurred. The surveyor's attention may therefore have to be directed to what it will cost to complete the work by another sub-contractor. This may mean that the negotiation for the completion of the sub-contract work will be on higher rates than the original quotation. There will be an advantage to the employer if the same sub-contractor can be persuaded to complete. Provided therefore the figure negotiated is no more than another sub-contractor could complete for then it can be accepted.

Bond

The contractor may be required to take out a bond for the due completion of the work and this is in the sum of 10% of the contract sum. Subject to its terms this can be used in the case of bankruptcy where the employer is put to additional expense through the contractor's bankruptcy. Bond-holders are sometimes banks, but more usually insurance companies specialising in this business. Although they may be liable for paying the employer such extra money as is necessary to complete the job, they have no control over the way the contract is completed. On the other hand it is up to the employer to complete it without any undue extravagance and it is just as well, to avoid future repercussions, to keep the bond-holder informed of what is happening.

One point of complexity arises concerning suppliers and sub-contractors. The contract gives the employer power to pay up outstanding amounts due to any supplier or sub-contractor (clause 25 (3) (b)). However, cases may arise where the effect of the employer exercising his right to make such payments falls, in fact, entirely on the bond-holder. Probably the bond-holder would have to pay up in such a case but he might object, at any rate, in the first instance.

Final account

Two final accounts have to be prepared when there has been a bankruptcy. The relevant clause in the contract is 25 (3) (d). The first or notional final account will be the amount which the contract would have cost had the first contractor completed in the ordinary way. This means that not only must all variations ordered before the bankruptcy be measured and priced at the rates relevant to the first contract, but also that all variations ordered on the completion contract must be included and priced at the rates which would have pertained had the first contract continued.

The second final account will be a normal final account for the completion contract and will only include those variations ordered during the completion contract.

" bankruptcy . . . is relatively infrequent "

79

They, of course, will be priced at the relevant prices and rates for the completion contract which may well be different from the first contract.

One point which needs to be watched is that if the completion contractor has to make good any defects which were caused by the bankrupt contractor and these are ordered as a variation on the completion contract, they should not show as a variation on the first final account because they would not have been included in that final account had the first contractor completed normally.

A point arises as to the extent of the variations ordered on the completion contract which can be taken into account on the first final account. Normal variations will go into account but where extras are exceptionally large or involve a change in the character of the job the trustee may have reasonable grounds for objection.

The statement showing the financial position of all the parties at completion is illustrated in the cases shown opposite.

In Case 1 it has been assumed that the contract was able to be completed without too much trouble and there is still something to come to the bankrupt contractor's trustee. It must be remembered that when the event of bankruptcy occurred there was probably considerable money in the retention fund and also, unless a certificate had been issued immediately before, there would be some money for work done but not yet certified. In Case 1 therefore it is assumed that the extra cost of completing the contract was less than the monies outstanding to the bankrupt contractor at the time of his bankruptcy and therefore there is finally a debt due from the employer to the trustee in bankruptcy.

In Case 2, however, it will be seen that the extra cost of completing the work was considerably greater than the money outstanding at the time of the bankruptcy. In this case the retention sum would have been relatively small as the contract was only one-third on.

In Case 2 if there were a bond for 10% of the contract sum, then the employer would, depending on the terms of the bond, first recover from the trustee the amount in the pound which was being paid out and would then get up to a maximum of £20,000 from the bond-holder. If the final dividend were 10p in the pound he would receive £3,030 from the trustee, leaving £27,270 of which the bond-holder would have to pay £20,000 reducing the employer's ultimate loss to £7,270. If, on the other hand the final dividend were 80p in the pound he would receive £24,240 from the trustee and the bond-holder would provide the balance of £6,060.

The agreement of the second final account creates no difficulty because there is a contractor's organisation with which to work. The first final account, however, will probably have to be done by the quantity surveyor alone and there will be very little opportunity for the bankrupt contractor to check it as his staff will probably be dispersed and no one will be available. The trustee in bankruptcy should be informed of the way the final account is being prepared and sent a copy at completion for his agreement.

Fees and other expenses

A bankruptcy will cause the employer to have to pay considerable extra fees and expenses. For example, the architect may well have had additional visits to the site, additional prints of drawings required and other expenses. The quantity surveyor will have had a great deal of extra measurement as well as the complication of sorting out two final accounts, etc. Furthermore the employer himself may have had to pay a watchman in the interim period between the bankruptcy and the completion contract

CASE 1 – *Resulting in debt from Employer to Contractor*

	£	£
Amount of original contract (with bankrupt contractor)....................		200,000
Additions (whether ordered with bankrupt contractor or completion contractor, but priced at rates in original contract)		10,000
		210,000
Omissions (same rules as for additions)		7,500
Amount of notional final account if original contractor had completed		202,500
Amount of completion contract	30,000	
Additions (for completion contract only and priced at relevant rates in the completion contract)	2,500	
	32,500	
Omissions (ditto)	2,000	
Amount of final account of completion contract	30,500	
Additional professional fees incurred....................................	1,500	
Amount certified and paid to bankrupt contract before bankruptcy............	169,000	201,000
Debt payable by employer to trustee in bankruptcy		£ 1,500

CASE 2. – *Resulting in debt from Contractor to Employer*

	£	£
Amount of original contract (with bankrupt contractor).....................		200,000
Additions (whether ordered with bankrupt contractor or completion contractor, but priced at rates in original contract)		10,000
		210,000
Omissions (same rules as for additions)		7,500
Amount of notional final account if original contractor had completed		202,500
Amount of completion contract	150,000	
Additions (for completion of contract only and priced at relevant rates in the completion contract)	10,500	
	160,500	
Omissions (ditto)	7,700	
Amount of final account of completion contract	152,800	
Additional professional fees incurred....................................	7,500	
Amount certified and paid to bankrupt contractor before bankruptcy..........	72,500	232,800
Debt payable by trustee in bankruptcy to employer		£ 30,300

81

starting. All these amounts can be charged against any sums which may be due from the employer to the trustee in bankruptcy. Further, where the final result indicates a debt due from the trustee in bankruptcy to the employer, this will be increased by the amount of the above expenses. The cases previously referred to only showed the position concerning the building contract and additional fees.

The following is a list of items which may be deducted from the notional final account:

(a) Direct payments to suppliers and sub-contractors.
(b) Amount of final account for completion contract.
(c) Cost of maintenance and remedial works in respect of work done by original contractor.
(d) Cost of additional insurances paid by employer.
(e) Cost of watching and lighting the works during period between default of original contractor and commencement of completion contract.
(f) Additional professional fees and expenses incurred by employer.
(g) Damages claimed by employer.

Bankruptcy of employer

In these circumstances the contractor may determine his own employment but as in the case of bankruptcy of the contractor the contract still remains. The only difference here is that the contractor's determination of his own employment is not automatic and he must give notice by registered post or recorded delivery to either employer or architect.

As far as the contract is concerned it is unlikely, of course, to proceed. The contractor becomes a creditor of the employer and the amount of the debt will be calculated in accordance with clause 26 (2) (b) of the conditions of contract which states that, after taking into account amounts previously paid the contractor should be paid:

(i) The total value of work completed at the date of determination.
(ii) The total value of work begun and executed but not completed at the date of determination, the value being ascertained in accordance with Clause 11 (4) of the conditions as if such work were a variation required by the Architect.
(iii) Any sum ascertained in respect of direct loss and/or expense under Clauses 11 (6), 24 and 34 (2) of the conditions (whether ascertained before or after the date of determination).
(iv) The cost of materials or goods properly ordered for works for which the contractor shall have paid or for which the Contractor is legally bound to pay, and on such payment by the Employer any materials or goods so paid for shall become the property of the Employer.
(v) The reasonable cost of removal from the site of temporary buildings, plant, tools, equipment, goods and materials which the Contractor is required to move under clause 26 (2) (a).
(vi) Any direct loss and/or damage caused to the Contractor by the determination.

Although, as will be seen from the above, materials on site paid for by the employer become the employer's property the contractor has a lien on them until payment of all debts from the employer to him. This is made clear in the contract, but there are some doubts as to whether such a lien would be enforceable against the trustee in bankruptcy in law.

The employment of the architect and quantity surveyor does not end with the employer's bankruptcy but they can seek undertakings from the trustee that they will be paid for their services before carrying on with their duties. If such undertakings are forthcoming they must then proceed with their respective duties in the winding up of the contract and the settlement of accounts, claims and so on.

If the trustee cannot give assurances as to payment of professional fees the architect and quantity surveyor cannot be forced to perform their duties for nothing and it will rest with the contractor to prepare the accounts unilaterally and negotiate direct with the trustee. The architect and quantity surveyor should, however, make any relevant documents available and give any reasonable assistance that they can in the circumstances.

Bankruptcy of a nominated sub-contractor

Unlike bankruptcy of a main contractor's own sub-contractor the situation in the event of bankruptcy of a nominated sub-contractor is rather different.

In Bickerton v N.W. Metropolitan Regional Hospital Board (1970) it was ruled in the House of Lords that, in the event of a nominated sub-contractor going into liquidation, and the liquidator refusing to carry on with the sub-contract, there is a duty by the architect to re-nominate and for the employer to bear any additional costs so incurred.

Almost inevitably, unless the liquidation takes place after nomination but before the sub-contractor has commenced work, delays on the project will occur. Any such delay will require the architect to grant an extension of time to the main contractor under clause 23 (g) provided he, the main contractor, has taken all reasonable steps to avoid or reduce the delay.

SUPPLEMENT – the 1980 Standard Form

INTRODUCTION

A list of contract documents published by the JCT in connection with the 1980 edition of the Standard Form of Building Contract follows at the end of this introduction.

We would like particularly to draw the attention of readers to the *JCT Guide* which has been published for the Joint Contracts Tribunal by RIBA Publications Ltd and which sets out the changes between the 1963 and 1980 editions and deals in some detail with the main changes and the new procedures. It is essential reading for anyone about to use the 1980 Standard Form for the first time.

The contents of the new Standard Form are listed at the beginning of each form as an index to the clause and sub-clause headings and the decimal numbering system has been adopted. The latter feature may be found confusing at first, but it is to be hoped that this is only due to unfamiliarity. However, one is bound to feel that it will be some time before 'clause 25.4.7' comes to mind as easily as its predecessor, 'clause 23(g)'.

The new layout which follows from the use of decimal numbering, however, does make for easier reading and in many respects makes the contract a more workable document.

The main changes which have taken place are in connection with extensions of time, payment and retention, the valuation of variations and the nomination of sub-contractors and suppliers. In addition the fluctuations clauses have been taken out of the main body of the conditions and have been extensively revised and clarified. The fluctuations clauses themselves, clauses 38, 39 and 40, are published as a separate document and incorporated in the conditions by reference in a short clause 37 and an entry in the Appendix.

The other new feature is a list of definitions which is set out in clause 1.3. These should be carefully studied before referring to the conditions themselves as these defined terms are used in the text. For example the various risks referred to in the 'fire insurance' clause, formerly clause 20 and now clause 22, are now collectively known as 'Clause 22 – Perils'. Similarly the various circumstances which entitle the contractor to apply for an extension of time, formerly listed in clause 23 and now set out in clause 25.4, are collectively known as 'Relevant Events'.

The 1980 Standard Form and its associated documents will no doubt be discussed and argued about at great length in the early days and in due course new editions of the various reference books on building contracts will emerge. Everyone involved in the administration of building contracts will gradually become more familiar with the new provisions and no doubt there will be disputes as to the interpretation of unfamiliar wording. We would exhort architects and quantity surveyors and indeed others connected with the contract to bear in mind that the biggest contribution that each person can make towards avoiding disputes is to do his job properly. We hope that this supplement to *Contract Administration* will help to set those concerned on the right course as the 1980 Standard Form comes into use.

List of Contract Documents issued by the JCT in connection with the 1980 Standard Form

Standard Form, Local Authorities, with Quantities, 1980 Edition.
Standard Form, Local Authorities, without Quantities, 1980 Edition.
Standard Form, Private, with Quantities, 1980 Edition.
Standard Form, Private, without Quantities, 1980 Edition.
Standard Form, Local Authorities, with Approximate Quantities, 1980 Edition.
Standard Form, Private, with Approximate Quantities, 1980 Edition.
Sectional Completion Supplement, 1980 Edition.
Fluctuations Clauses for use with the Local Authorities editions with Quantities, without Quantities and with Approximate Quantities.
Fluctuations Clauses for use with the Private editions with Quantities, without Quantities and with Approximate Quantities.
Tender NSC/1 – Standard Form of Nominated Sub-Contract Tender and Agreement.
Agreement NSC/2 – Standard Form of Employer/Nominated Sub-Contractor Agreement.
Agreement NSC/2a – Agreement NSC/2 adapted for use where Tender NSC/1 has not been used.
Nomination NSC/3 – Standard Form for Nomination of a Sub-Contractor where Tender NSC/1 has been used.
Sub-Contract NSC/4 – Standard Form of Sub-Contract for Sub-Contractors who have tendered on Tender NSC/1 and executed Agreement NSC/2 and been nominated by Nomination NSC/3.
Sub-Contract NSC/4a – Sub-Contract NSC/4 adapted for use where Tender NSC/1, Agreement NSC/2 and Nomination NSC/3 have not been used.
Fluctuations Clauses for use with NSC/4 and NSC/4a.
Formula Rules for use with the Standard Forms of Contract and Nominated Sub-Contracts.
Form of Tender for Nominated Suppliers.

JCT Guide to the Standard Form of Building Contract, 1980 Edition.

The JCT also issues forms for design and build contracts and for minor works.

Main Clause Headings of the 1980 Standard Form
(cross-referenced to 1963 edition)

ARTICLES OF AGREEMENT

CONDITIONS: PART 1

Clause	GENERAL	Equivalent clause in 1963 edition
1	Interpretation, definitions etc.	–
2	Contractor's obligations	1 & 12 (part)
3	Contract sum – additions or deductions – adjustment – interim certificates	–
4	Architect's/supervising officer's instructions	2
5	Contract documents – other documents – issue of certificates	3
6	Statutory obligations, notices, fees and charges	4

CONDITIONS: PART 2
NOMINATED SUB-CONTRACTORS AND
NOMINATED SUPPLIERS

CONDITIONS: PART 3
FLUCTUATIONS

APPENDIX
SUPPLEMENTAL PROVISIONS (the VAT Agreement)

1: THE BUILDING TEAM

(See also Chapter 1: pages 3–7)

The 1980 Standard Form does not materially change the roles of the various members of the building team, but it does spell out in more detail their respective rights, duties and liabilities and some of the previously implied duties are now mandatory.

The rights, duties and responsibilities of the respective members of the team are listed below. For simplicity, clause references have been given to the first decimal number only.

The employer

Articles   Name and address
Appointment of architect
Status under statutory tax deduction scheme
Rights, liabilities and procedure in respect of arbitration

Clause

4.1	Right to employ others if contractor does not comply with instructions
5.1	Custody of contract documents (Local Authorities edition only)
5.7	Duties in relation to confidential nature of contract documents
12	Right to appoint clerk of works
18.1	Procedure as to partial possession by the employer
19.1	Rights as to assignment of contract
19.3	Rights and procedure as to sub-letting by contractor
20 **21**	Rights, duties and liabilities as to insurance
22A	Rights when insurance against fire and other perils is responsibility of contractor
22B	Duty to insure works against fire and other perils
22C	Duty to insure works and existing structures against fire and other perils
23.1	Duty to give contractor possession of site
24.2	Right to deduct damages in respect of non-completion
27.1	Right to determine contract on contractor's default
27.4	Rights and duties in event of determination of contractor's default or bankruptcy
28.2	Rights and duties in event of determination of contract by contractor
29	Rights and duties in respect of work on site not forming part of contract
30.1	Duty to pay contractor within 14 days of issue of interim certificate Right to make deductions from monies due
30.4	Right to hold retention in interim payments

17.2
17.3 } Duties and rights as to making good defects
17.4
17.5

18.1   Duties and procedure as to partial possession by the employer
19.1   Rights as to assignment of contract

19.2
19.3 } Rights and procedure as to sub-letting
19.4

19A   Duties in regard to fair wages (Local Authorities edition only)
20.1   Liabilities in respect of injury to persons
20.2   Liabilities in respect of damage to property
21   Duties regarding general insurance
22A   Duty to insure works against fire and other perils
22B } Duties and rights when insurance against fire and other perils is
22C } responsibility of employer
23.1   Duty to proceed diligently with the works
24.2   Liability for damages in event of non-completion
25.2   Duty to give notice to architect and sub-contractors of delays; and information to be given
25.3   Duty to prevent delay
26.1   Right to recover loss and expense incurred by matters materially affecting progress of the works
         Duties as to notification and information to be provided
26.4   Duties in respect of claims by nominated sub-contractors
27.4   Rights and duties in event of determination of contract by employer
28.1   Right to determine contract and grounds for determination
28.2   Rights and duties in event of determination
29   Rights and duties in respect of work on site not forming part of contract
30.1   Right to payment under interim certificate within 14 days
30.3   Duties in respect of off-site materials included in interim certificates
30.5   Right to require employer to place retention money in separate bank account (Private edition only)
30.6   Duty to provide documents necessary for adjusting the contract sum
         Right to receive copy of computation of adjusted contract sum
31   Duties in connection with statutory tax deduction scheme (where employer is a 'contractor')
35.2   Right to tender for sub-contract works
35.4   Right to object to nominated sub-contractor
35.5– } Procedure and duties regarding proposed nomination of sub-contractors by
35.10 } basic method
35.11 } Ditto by alternative method
35.12 }
35.13   Duty to discharge interim payments to nominated sub-contractors
         Duty to provide proof of payments to nominated sub-contractors
35.24   Duties in connection with re-nomination after default or determination by sub-contractor
         Duty to obtain instruction before determination of nominated sub-contract

38.4 } Duty to give written notice of fluctuations and to provide evidence of same
38.5 } and computations

Supplemental
Provisions   Rights and duties in regard to VAT

The architect
Articles Name and address
          Duties and procedure in respect of arbitration

Clause

2.3	Duty as to discrepancies between documents
3	Duty to include ascertained amounts in interim certificates
4.2	Duty to justify instructions
4.3	Duty to issue instructions in writing
	Procedure in connection with verbal instructions
5.1	Custody of contract documents (Private edition only)

5.2
5.3 } Duties concerning furnishing copies of drawings and documents
5.4

5.6	Right to require return of drawings on completion
5.7	Duties in relation to confidential nature of contract documents
5.8	Procedure for issue of architect's certificates
6.1	Duty to issue instructions in connection with statutory requirements
7	Duties as to setting-out
8.2	Right to require proof of standards of materials etc.
8.3	Rights as to opening up of suspect work
8.4	Rights as to removal of faulty work
8.5	Right to order exclusion of persons from the works
11	Right of access to job and workshops
13.2	Right to issue instruction requiring a variation
13.3	Duty to issue instructions regarding provisional sums
16.1	Rights regarding removal of unfixed goods
17.1	Duty to issue certificate of practical completion

17.2
17.3
17.4 } Duties as to defects
17.5

18.1	Duties concerning partial possession by the employer

19.2
19.3 } Duties and procedure as to sub-letting by contractor

21.1	Right to require evidence of insurance by contractor
21.2	Duties in regard to insurances covered by provisional sums
22	Duties and rights in connection with insurances against fire and other perils
23.2	Rights regarding postponement of work
24.1	Duty to issue certificates in event of non-completion
25.3	Duty to grant extensions of time and to fix new completion date; information to be given

26.1 Duty to ascertain loss and expense incurred by contractor
26.3 Duty to give details of extension of time granted
26.4 Similar duties in respect of nominated sub-contractors
27.1 Procedure for determining contract on behalf of employer
27.4 Duties in event of determination of contract by employer
30.1 Duty to issue interim certificates
30.3 Discretion to include off-site materials in interim certificate
30.5 Duty to prepare and issue statements of retention in respect of each interim certificate
30.6 Duty to inform contractor and sub-contractors of final valuations of work of nominated sub-contractors
30.7 Duty to issue interim certificate including all final amounts due to nominated sub-contractors
30.8 Duty to issue final certificate and to inform each nominated sub-contractor of date of issue
32 Duties in connection with determination of contract in event of war
33 Rights concerning war damage
34 Duties relating to antiquities found on site
35.5–
35.10 } Procedure and duties for nomination of sub-contractor by basic method
35.11
35.12 } Ditto by alternative method
35.13 Duties regarding interim payments to nominated sub-contractors
35.14 Duty to operate provisions of sub-contract in dealing with applications for extensions of time
35.15 Duty to certify if nominated sub-contractor fails to complete in time
35.16 Duty to certify practical completion by nominated sub-contractor
35.17
35.18 } Duties regarding early final payment to nominated sub-contractor
35.23 Duties when proposed nomination does not proceed
35.24 Duty to re-nominate if sub-contractor defaults or determines sub-contract
35.25 Duties in connection with determination of sub-contract
36.2 } Duty, subject to conditions, to issue instructions regarding nominated
36.4 } suppliers

The quantity surveyor

Articles   Name and address

Clause

5.1 Custody of contract documents (Private edition only)
5.7 Duties as to confidential nature of contract documents
13.4 Duty to value variations
13.5 Rules for valuing variations
26.1 Duty to ascertain loss and expense incurred by contractor, if so instructed
26.4 Similar duty in respect of nominated sub-contractors
30.1 Duty to make valuations for interim certificates when required
30.5 Duty to prepare statement of retention in respect of each interim certificate if so instructed

The person-in-charge

Clause

The clerk of works

Clause

2: PLACING THE CONTRACT

(See also Chapter 2: pages 8–15)

Under the 1980 Standard Form the contract documents consist, as previously, of the Articles of Agreement, drawings showing the extent and nature of the work, and the bills of quantities.

The Articles of Agreement have been revised in both format and content. The recitals are now numbered and include reference to the status of the employer for the purposes of the statutory tax deduction scheme. This requires a statement in the Appendix to the Conditions of Contract indicating whether or not the employer is a 'contractor' for the purpose of the scheme. Articles 1–4 are unchanged apart from drafting amendments and these require the insertion of the contract sum, the name and address of the architect, or alternatively in the Local Authorities edition the supervising officer, and the name and address of the quantity surveyor.

Article 5 is new and comprises the Arbitration Agreement which was previously contained in the Conditions. In the normal course of events Article 5 requires no insertions or deletions, but there is a footnote regarding amendments if the law of the contract is not be English law.

In the Conditions of Contract there are several clauses which need to be considered with a view to deletions or other amendments being made. These are summarized below.

Clause **5.3.1.2** Under this clause the contractor is required to provide the architect with copies of his master programme for the execution of the works and subsequently to amend it in the event of an extension of time being granted.
If this is not required this clause should be deleted and in the following clause, 5.3.2, the words in parenthesis which refer to the master programme should also be deleted. We would however draw attention to our comments on this subject in section 3.

Clause **22A, 22B, 22C** Two of these clauses must be deleted, according to whether the employer or the contractor is responsible for insurance against fire and other risks, now known as 'Clause 22 Perils'.
There is a reminder in a footnote to these clauses that it is sometimes not possible to obtain insurance against certain of the clause 22 perils which are, incidentally, set out in the definitions contained in clause 1.3 of the Conditions. If certain perils have to be excluded the clause must be amended accordingly.

Clause **35.13.5.4.4** This clause will require amendment as indicated in the footnote in the rather unlikely event of a nominated sub-contractor being an individual or a company not incorporated under the Companies Acts.

Completion of the Appendix, the Supplemental Provisions covering VAT and, if applicable, the Sectional Completion Supplement will follow similar lines to those which have applied with the previous Standard Form. Particular attention is drawn to the additional information now to be given in the Appendix which is as follows:

CONTRACT ADMINISTRATION

The employer's status for the purpose of the statutory tax deduction scheme.

Whether or not the joinder provisions in respect of arbitration set out in articles 5.1.4 and 5.1.5 are to apply.

Which alternative applies for fluctuations.

3: PROGRESS AND SITE MEETINGS

(See also Chapter 3: pages 16–21)

Programme

Clause 5.3.1.2 of the 1980 Standard Form states that as soon as possible after the execution of the contract the contractor shall provide the architect with two copies of his master programme for the execution of the works. This is an innovation as far as the contract conditions are concerned, but it is in fact only incorporating into the conditions a procedure which has normally been regarded as good practice for many years. The clause appears to assume that the contractor will have a master programme and if he does not have one he presumably cannot be obliged to prepare one. If a programme is required, therefore, this should be stated in the bills of quantities.

The master programme is not a contract document and clause 5.3.2 makes it clear that nothing contained in the programme can impose any obligation on the contractor beyond the obligations imposed by the contract documents as such.

In addition to providing the master programme at the start of the contract the contractor is also required to update it within 14 days of any decision by the architect to fix a new completion date for the contract.

Footnotes in the conditions indicate that clause 5.3.1.2 may be deleted and clause 5.3.2 amended if no master programme is required. This should not be regarded as making the clause an optional one as experience has shown that a master programme is an essential tool of management both for the contractor and for the architect. Only in exceptional circumstances would a master programme not be required; indeed in many cases there is much to be said for contractors tendering being required to submit the master programme with their tenders.

Sub-contracts

The new procedures and disciplines imposed by the 1980 Standard Form in connection with the selection and nomination of sub-contractors are among the most radical changes made in the conditions of contract. The procedure for obtaining tenders for nominated sub-contractors' work is dealt with in detail in chapter 7 of the sixth edition of *Pre-Contract Practice* and the procedure for nomination is dealt with later in this addendum in section 5, 'Architect's Instructions'. It is sufficient to say here that it is perhaps now even more important at the initial site meeting to clarify the position regarding all work which will be the subject of nomination.

4: SITE SUPERVISION

(See also Chapter 4: pages 22–32)

The procedures described in this section will not be affected by the 1980 Standard Form.

5: INSTRUCTIONS AND VARIATIONS

(See also Chapter 5: pages 33–42)

Architect's instructions

The right of the contractor to question the architect's power to issue an instruction is embodied in clause 4.2 of the 1980 Standard Form. Following are the matters in respect of which the architect is empowered by the conditions of contract to issue instructions.

Clause

2.3	Discrepancies in documents
6.1.3	Compliance with statutory requirements
7	Levels and setting out the works
8.3	Opening up work for inspection
8.4	Removal of work, materials or goods not in accordance with the contract
8.5	Exclusion from the works of any person employed thereon
13.2	Variations as defined in clause 13.1
13.3.1	Expenditure of provisional sums included in the contract bills
13.3.2	Expenditure of provisional sums included in a sub-contract
17.2 **17.3**	Making good defects, shrinkage and other faults
23.2	Postponement of the execution of any works
32.2	Protection of the work in the event of war
33.1.2	Action in the event of war damage
34.2	Action in the event of antiquities being found
35.5.2	Application of alternative method of nominating a sub-contractor in lieu of the basic method
35.8	Action in the event of the contractor being unable to reach agreement with proposed nominated sub-contractor
35.9	Action in the event of proposed nominated sub-contractor withdrawing his tender
35.10.2	Nomination of sub-contractor under the basic method
35.11.2	Nomination of sub-contractor under the alternative method
35.18.1.1	Nomination of a substituted sub-contractor in the event of a nominated sub-contractor failing to rectify defects
35.23	Omission of work for which it was proposed to nominate a sub-contractor or nomination of an alternative sub-contractor if the proposed nomination does not proceed
35.24.4	Procedure following contractor's application to determine a nominated sub-contract as a result of the sub-contractor's default; and subsequent re-nomination

35.24.5 Re-nomination in the event of a nominated sub-contractor's bankruptcy

35.24.6 Re-nomination in the event of a nominated sub-contractor determining the sub-contract

The procedure for issuing instructions has not changed under the 1980 Form, but greater emphasis has been given to the requirement that all architect's instructions must be in writing.

"all instructions issued by the architect shall be issued in writing"

Variations

The 'variation' has been defined in tabulated form in clause 13 and this definition is set out below.

13.1 The term 'variation' as used in the conditions means:

13.1 .1 the alteration or modification of the design, quality or quantity of the works as shown upon the contract drawings and described by or referred to in the contract bills, including:

.1 .1 the addition, omission or substitution of any work;

.1 .2 the alteration of the kind or standard of any of the materials or goods to be used in the works;

13.1 .1 .3 the removal from the site of any work executed or materials or goods brought thereon by the contractor for the purpose of the works other than work materials or goods which are not in accordance with this contract;

13.1 .2 the addition, alteration or omission of any obligations or restrictions imposed by the employer in the contract bills in regard to:

.2 .1 access to the site or use of any specific parts of the site;

.2 .2 limitations of working space;

.2 .3 limitations of working hours;

.2 .4 the execution or completion of the work in any specific order;

but excludes:

13.1 .3 nomination of a sub-contractor to supply and fix materials or goods or to execute work of which the measured quantities have been set out and priced by the contractor in the contract bills for supply and fixing or execution by the contractor.

The matters set out in clause 13.1.1 are similar to those in the 1963 Form, but those in 13.1.2 are new. It will be seen that these relate to some of the obligations and restrictions imposed by the employer, particulars of which will have been set out in the bills of quantities in accordance with clause B.8 of the Standard Method of Measurement. It should be noted, however, that, while clause 4.1.1. requires the contractor to comply forthwith with all architect's instructions, those requiring a variation within the meaning of clause 13.1.2 are excepted from that general obligation.

Clearly an architect's instruction requiring a variation in respect of the matters referred to in clause 13.1.2 could materially affect the operation of the whole contract as far as the contractor is concerned. If the contractor considers this to be the case he would not be obliged to comply with the instruction immediately. Should this situation arise the contractor would have to set out in writing his reasons for objecting to the instruction and there would have to be a separate agreement as to how the changes in the obligations and the restrictions imposed by the employer are to be dealt with. Any adjustment to the contract sum would then be made in accordance with that agreement and not dealt with as a variation under the contract. If the parties are unable to reach agreement on the matter it could then be referred to arbitration, article 5.2.3 making provision for such a dispute to be arbitrated upon immediately.

Architect's instructions nominating sub-contractors and suppliers are covered by clauses 35.10.2 and 36.2 respectively and are dealt with in more detail later in this section. It should be noted that clause 13.1.3 precludes the architect from issuing an instruction nominating a sub-contractor to carry out work which has been measured in the bills of quantities and priced by the contractor as general contractor's work. If the architect wishes to do this he may do so only with the contractor's agreement. If the contractor does agree, arrangements for his profit, attendance on the sub-contractor and any other financial matters should be settled before the nomination is made.

Clause 13.3 requires the architect to issue instructions in regard to the expenditure of provisional sums in either the main contract bills or in any sub-contract.

Nomination of sub-contractors

Probably the most substantial change in the 1980 Standard Form is in connection with the nomination of sub-contractors. The new procedures now required to effect a nomination, together with the paperwork which accompanies them, may seem on the face of it to be cumbersome and long-winded. This is not in fact the case. The new provisions have been drawn up with a view to eliminating the many problems which have arisen in the past as a result of nominations being made on the basis of inadequate information and with little regard for the impact of the nomination on the programme and working arrangements of the general contractor. Professional advisers who have given proper attention to these matters in the past will have little difficulty in adopting the new procedures and should welcome the comprehensive documentation which has now been prepared in conjunction with the 1980 Standard Form.

A nominated sub-contractor is now defined as a sub-contractor whose selection is reserved to the architect. The architect may make his nomination in one of two ways, namely by the basic method using the full documentation, or by the alternative method which is a shorter procedure intended for use in the case of some of the minor items of work for which the architect may wish to nominate the sub-contractor.

Because of the importance of ensuring that the nominated sub-contractor's work can properly be integrated into the work of the main contractor, it is essential that decisions are taken in good time before tenders are invited. The preparatory work leading to a nomination ought, therefore, to be dealt with in the pre-contract stage and the detailed procedures under both the basic and the alternative methods are described in some detail in chapter 7 of the sixth edition of *Pre-Contract Practice for Architects or Quantity Surveyors*. It is not proposed to deal with the matter in detail again in this book, but it may be helpful to summarize here the sequence of events leading up to the nomination.

The basic method involves the use of the Form of Tender and Agreement (NSC/1), the Employer/Nominated Sub-Contractor Agreement (NSC/2), the Form of Nomination (NSC/3) and the Standard Form of Sub-Contract (NSC/4). The procedure is as follows:

- The architect prepares Tender NSC/1, inserting in schedule 1 the particulars of the main contract.
- At the same time the architect prepares the Agreement NSC/2.
- The architect sends the original and two copies of NSC/1 and the original NSC/2 to the proposed sub-contractor.
- The proposed sub-contractor completes Tender NSC/1 and the two copies and signs on page 1.
- The proposed sub-contractor executes Agreement NSC/2 under hand or under seal as instructed by the architect.
- The proposed sub-contractor returns to the architect the original documents and the copies of NSC/1.
- The architect signs the Tender NSC/1 and the two copies on page 1 as 'approved' on behalf of the employer.
- The employer executes Agreement NSC/2 again either under hand or under seal, retaining the original and sending the architect a certified true copy.
- The architect sends to the proposed sub-contractor the certified copy of the agreement.
- The architect sends the main contractor a preliminary notice of nomination, accompanied by the original Tender NSC/1 and its two copies as then

completed, together with a copy of the Agreement NSC/2 for the main contractor's information.

- The main contractor checks that the details in schedule 1 of Tender NSC/1 are correct.
- The main contractor completes schedule 2 insofar as it has not already been completed by the proposed sub-contractor, deleting those items which are no longer relevant and agreeing all the remaining items with the sub-contractor.
- The contractor and the sub-contractor sign schedule 2 and the contractor signs the tender itself to indicate his acceptance of it, subject only to the architect issuing the nomination instruction.
- The contractor then returns the original, and now completed, Tender NSC/1 and the copies to the architect.
- The architect issues his instruction to the contractor nominating the proposed sub-contractor using Nomination NSC/3, sending with it the original Tender NSC/1.
- At the same time the architect sends to the proposed sub-contractor a copy of Nomination NSC/3, together with a certified copy of the completed Tender NSC/1.
- The contractor and the nominated sub-contractor enter into a Sub-Contract NSC/4. Whether this will be under hand or under seal will have been stated previously in schedule 2 of Tender NSC/1.

Under the alternative method the Tender NSC/1 and Nomination NSC/3 are dispensed with; the Employer/Sub-Contractor Agreement is optional, but where required NSC/2a is used in place of NSC/2; and the Standard Form of Sub-Contract NSC/4a is used in place of NSC/4.

If it is proposed to use the alternative method this must have been stated in the bills of quantities or in the architect's instruction under which the nomination was made. At the same time it must be stated whether or not the Agreement NSC/2a is to be entered into. The architect may, however, issue an instruction substituting the alternative method for the basic method, or the basic method for the alternative method, but any such instruction must be issued before the preliminary notice of nomination. Such an instruction would be treated as a variation.

In the event of the contractor and the sub-contractor being unable to agree on the particular conditions to be inserted in schedule 2 of Tender NSC/1 the contractor must inform the architect in writing, giving reasons for their inability to reach agreement. The architect must then issue such instructions as may be necessary. Similarly if the sub-contractor withdraws his offer at this stage, the contractor must inform the architect in writing and await the architect's instructions. In such circumstances the architect must either make a fresh nomination or issue an instruction requiring as a variation the omission of the work concerned. In such a case he may, of course, require a further variation that the work be carried out by the general contractor.

The contractor does, of course, still have the right to make a reasonable objection to a nominated sub-contractor and if he wishes to make such an objection the contract requires him to do so at the earliest practicable moment and in any case not later than when he returns Tender NSC/1 to the architect. If the alternative method of nomination applies, under which NSC/1 is not used, then the contractor must make his objection within 7 days of receiving the architect's instruction nominating the sub-contractor.

It must always be borne in mind that a sub-contractor may only be nominated for work covered by a p.c. sum in the bills of quantities, or where the sub-contractor is named in the bills or in an instruction regarding the expenditure of a provisional sum, or, subject to certain qualifications, in a variation order.

If after nomination a sub-contractor defaults in his performance of the contract, or if he goes into liquidation, the architect must make a fresh nomination. Clause 35.24 sets out the procedure to be followed in such circumstances. As this is not a very common occurrence it is not proposed to enlarge on those procedures here, but they should of course be carefully followed when such a situation arises.

Nomination of suppliers

A supplier is nominated or deemed to be nominated if the supply of materials or goods is covered by a p.c. sum in the bills and the supplier is either named in the bills or subsequently named by the architect in his instruction regarding the expenditure of the p.c. sum; or where in an instruction regarding the expenditure of a provisional sum or in a variation order the architect specifies materials or goods which can only be purchased from one supplier. In the latter case the materials or goods concerned must be made the subject of a p.c. sum in the architect's instruction or the variation order.

Clause 36 requires the architect to issue instructions for the purpose of nominating a supplier for any materials or goods covered by a p.c. sum and the clause sets out the manner in which the costs to be set against the p.c. sum are to be ascertained.

Clause 36.4 sets out the conditions of sale which the supplier will be required to accept in his contract of sale with the contractor and if the supplier refuses to accept those conditions the contractor cannot be required to accept the nomination.

Valuing variations

The contract provides that variations and work carried out by the contractor in expenditure of provisional sums shall be valued by the quantity surveyor and clause 13.5 comprises the rules to be observed in making the valuation. There are several significant changes from previous editions of the Standard Form and the rules as they now stand may be summarized as follows:

—Work which can be properly valued by measurement:
   —Work similar to that set out in the contract bills, executed under similar conditions and with no significant change in the total quantity shall be valued at bill rates.
   —Work of a similar character to that set out in the contract bills but not executed under similar conditions or where there is a significant change in quantity shall be valued at rates pro rata to those in the contract bills, a fair allowance being made for the differences in conditions and/or quantity.
   —Work not similar to that set out in the contract bills shall be valued at fair rates and prices.
—Omissions shall be valued at the rates and prices contained in the bills.
—When valuing the foregoing the following must be taken into account:
   —Measurement must be in accordance with the method of measurement used for the preparation of the bills of quantities.
   —Allowance must be made for any percentage or lump sum adjustment in the contract bills.

—If appropriate, allowance must be made for any addition to or reduction of preliminaries.
—Work which cannot be properly valued by measurement shall be valued on a daywork basis.
—If any variation substantially changes the conditions under which other work is executed then that other work shall be revalued as if it was itself a variation.
—If the variation does not involve additional or substituted work or straightforward omissions, or if the valuation cannot reasonably be effected by the application of these valuation rules, then a fair valuation must be made.

It will be seen that it is now quite clear that if a variation causes either a change in the working conditions or a significant change in the quantities or in the conditions under which other work is carried out, then such changes must be taken into account in the valuation.

It is also quite clear that allowance must be made in valuing variations for percentage or lump sum adjustments which have been made in the contract bills and, where appropriate, an adjustment must be made in respect of preliminaries

The one matter which is no longer to be taken into account when valuing variations is any effect which the variation may have had on the regular progress of the work, or any direct loss and/or expense which the contractor may have incurred as a result of the variation but which he is unable to recover through the valuation or any other provision of the contract. These matters are now dealt with under clause 26.

The value of variations on sub-contract works, including the valuation of work carried out against provisional sums included in the sub-contract, is to be made in accordance with the relevant provisions of the sub-contract. The valuation rules in the sub-contract conditions are similar in principle to those of the main contract referred to above and it is not proposed to deal with them further here. In this connection, however, the 1980 Standard Form does clarify the position when the main contractor tenders for sub-contract works and his tender is accepted. Any variations in the sub-contract works are then valued in accordance with the terms of the sub-contract, not in accordance with the terms of the main contract.

6: INTERIM CERTIFICATES AND RETENTION

(See also Chapter 6: page 43–57)

As in the 1963 edition of the Standard Form, clause 30 in the 1980 Form deals with certificates and payments. However, the clause has been extensively revised, particularly in relation to retention.

General obligations

The general obligations of the parties are unchanged and the architect is still required to issue interim certificates at the periods stated in the appendix to the conditions, normally one month. After the certificate of practical completion has been issued the architect must continue to issue interim certificates as and when further amounts are ascertained as payable to the contractor, but in such cases the only proviso as to timing is that no interim certificate shall be issued within one month of the previous interim certificate. These provisions regarding the interim certificates after practical completion continue after the end of the defects liability period and after the issue of the certificate of completion of making good defects, until such time as the final account has been settled and the architect is in a position to issue the final certificate.

As soon as the final accounts of all the nominated sub-contractors have been ascertained, and in any case not less than 28 days before the issue of the final certificate, the architect must issue an interim certificate which includes the final amounts due to all nominated sub-contractors. This interim certificate can be issued within one month of the previous interim certificate. This is a new provision which will enable all payments to sub-contractors to be cleared before the final certificate, which will then include only the outstanding amounts due to the contractor.

The employer must pay the contractor any amounts due under a certificate within 14 days from the date of issue of the certificate; and the contractor in turn must pay any monies due to nominated sub-contractors within 17 days of the date of issue of the interim certificate by the architect.

When issuing his certificate the architect must direct the contractor as to the amounts including for nominated sub-contractors and must notify each nominated sub-contractor of the amount included. As will be seen later in this chapter the new rules regarding retention also require that at each interim certificate a statement shall be prepared specifying separately the amount of retention on the main contractor's work and on each nominated sub-contractor's work and that copies of that statement must be issued by the architect to the employer, the contractor and to each nominated sub-contractor involved.

Interim valuations

If clause 40 applies for fluctuations, that is using the price adjustment formulae, interim valuations must be prepared by the quantity surveyor prior to the issue of each interim certificate. If clauses 38 or 39 apply for fluctuations it is at the architect's discretion as to whether or not interim valuations are prepared by the quantity surveyor. In practice it is normal for such valuations to be prepared regardless of the way in which fluctuations are adjusted and again, although it is not a contractual requirement, it is normal practice for the contractor to co-operate with the quantity surveyor in preparing the valuations. This all follows long-established procedure and has not been changed by the 1980 Standard Form. However, the ascertainment of amounts due in interim certificates has now been re-defined.

The gross value to be included in interim certificates is now spelt out under two headings and may be summarized as follows:

Amounts to be included which are subject to retention:
1. The total value of the main contract works properly executed including variations and, where applicable, adjustment in respect of fluctuations where the price adjustment formula applies.
2. The total value of materials and goods delivered to or adjacent to the works.
3. The total value of materials and goods off site if authorized by the architect.
4. In respect of each nominated sub-contractor the total value of the sub-contract works, materials and goods as set out in 1–3 above for the main contract works.
5. The profit of the contractor upon the total amount included for each nominated sub-contractor including the sub-contractor's fluctuations and any other monies due to the sub-contractor under the terms of his sub-contract.

Amounts to be included which are not subject to retention:
1. Any amount which may become due to the contractor under the terms of the contract in respect of statutory fees and charges, setting out the works, opening up and testing, royalties, remedial works where the architect authorizes payment, and insurances under clause 21.2.3 (formerly 19(2)(a)).
2. Any amount due to the contractor by way of reimbursement for loss and expense arising from matters materially affecting the regular progress of the works or from the discovery of antiquities.
3. Any final payment to a nominated sub-contractor.
4. Any amount payable to the contractor in respect of fluctuations, other than those calculated by the price adjustment formula.
5. Any amount properly payable to a nominated sub-contractor in respect of statutory fees and charges, remedial works for which the architect authorizes payment, and fluctuations other than where the price adjustment formula applies.

If under the fluctuations provisions, other than where the price adjustment formula applies, there should be any sum payable by the contractor to the employer or by a nominated sub-contractor to the contractor, then such sum must be deducted from the amounts due in an interim certificate which are not subject to retention.

The inclusion in the gross value of an interim certificate of off-site materials or goods is at the discretion of the architect. Where such goods are included certain conditions must apply in order to safeguard the employer's interest in them. These conditions are set out in clause 30.3 and it is the architect's responsibility to ensure that those conditions have been complied with before he authorizes payment.

The gross valuation for an interim certificate comprises the total amounts which are subject to retention, plus the total amounts which are not subject to retention, less any amount allowable to the employer in respect of fluctuations all as summarized above. From this gross valuation there will be deducted retention and the total amounts stated as due in interim certificates previously issued.

Retention

The 1980 Standard Form states that the retention percentage shall be 5% unless a lower rate shall have been agreed between the parties and specified in the appendix to the conditions. A footnote recommends that where the contract sum is £500,000 or over the retention percentage should not exceed 3%.

Arrangements for the partial release of retention have been changed and this no longer depends upon the issue by the architect of a certificate of practical completion in respect of the whole or part of the works. To apply the contractual provisions for the deduction of retention, therefore, it is necessary to divide the value of the work included in each interim certificate into three parts:

- Total value of work which has not yet reached practical completion plus unfixed materials and goods — subject to full retention
- Total value of work which has reached practical completion but for which a certificate of completion of making good defects has not been issued — subject to half retention
- Total value of work for which a certificate of completion of making good defects has been issued — nil retention

These provisions apply equally to work carried out by nominated sub-contractors the value of which is, of course, included in the gross valuation. In the case of nominated sub-contractors there will now be in the normal course of events the additional obligation on the employer to make early final payment to the nominated sub-contractor in accordance with the provisions of clause 35.17 of the Standard Form. That obligation arises under the terms of the Employer/Nominated Sub-Contractor Agreement (NSC/2 or NSC/2a), which now forms part of the standard documentation required for the nomination of the sub-contractor.

Clause 35.16 states that when in the opinion of the architect practical completion of the works executed by a nominated sub-contractor is achieved he shall forthwith issue a certificate to that effect and practical completion of such works shall be deemed to have taken place on the day named in that certificate. Clause 35.17 states that where the Agreement NSC/2 or NSC/2a has been entered into and the relevant clauses of the Agreement are unamended, then at any time after the date of practical completion of the sub-contract works the architect may, and on the expiry of 12 months from the date of practical completion must, include in an interim certificate the final payment to the nominated sub-contractor, subject to the sub-contractor having remedied any defects and having sent to the architect or the quantity surveyor all documents necessary for the final adjustment of the sub-contract sum.

This means that the retention in respect of each nominated sub-contractor must be separately identified in the valuation for the interim certificate.

This separate identification of retention monies is also necessary to enable the employer's obligations regarding retention monies to be fulfilled.

Those obligations are set out in the rules on the treatment of retention contained in clause 30.5 of the Standard Form. These rules state:

1. That the employer's interest in retention is fiduciary as a trustee for the contractor and for any nominated sub-contractor, but without an obligation to invest. In other words it is money held by the employer on trust.
2. That at the date of each interim certificate the architect or the quantity surveyor shall prepare a statement specifying the amount of retention for the contractor and for each nominated sub-contractor, copies of that statement being issued by the architect to the employer, the contractor and each nominated sub-contractor.
3. That the employer shall at the request of the contractor or any nominated sub-contractor place the retention money in a separate bank account and certify to the architect, with a copy to the contractor, that the retention has been so placed (this rule does not apply in the Local Authorities edition of the Standard Form).
4. Where the employer excercises his right to deduct monies due to him under the terms of the contract from monies certified as being due to the contractor he may make such a deduction from amounts payable under a certificate, including any retention released in the certificate, but he cannot take into account retentions still held. If a deduction is made the employer must inform the contractor of the reasons for it, and if the deduction is from retention he must state the amount he has deducted from the contractor's share of the retention or from any nominated sub-contractor's share.

Payments to nominated sub-contractors

As indicated above the architect must direct the contractor as to the amount included in an interim certificate for each nominated sub-contractor and he must at the same time inform the sub-contractors concerned. The contractor must discharge his payment to the sub-contractor with 17 days of the date of issue of the certificate.

The new procedures for the nomination of sub-contractors, incorporating as they do the Employer/Nominated Sub-Contractor Agreement, impose stronger disciplines to be observed by all concerned in this payment process.

Before the issue of each interim certificate the contractor must provide the architect with reasonable proof that he has made any payments to nominated sub-contractors due under previous certificates. If he is unable to provide such proof then the procedures for direct payment set out below will apply, unless the contractor is able to satisfy the architect that the absence of proof is due to some failure or omission of the nominated sub-contractor concerned.

The procedure for direct payment is mandatory on the employer if the Employer/Nominated Sub-Contractor Agreement (NSC/2 or NSC/2a) has been entered into. Otherwise it is optional at the employer's discretion.

If the reasonable proof of payment is not forthcoming the architect must issue a certificate to that effect stating the amount in respect of which the contractor has failed to provide such proof. He must send a copy of that certificate to the nominated sub-contractor concerned.

Provided the certificate referred to above has been issued, the amount of any future payment to the contractor will be reduced by the amount by which the contractor has defaulted in his payment to the nominated sub-contractor and the employer will pay the sub-contractor concerned direct.

That direct payment will be made at the same time that the employer makes his payment to the contractor under the next interim certificate. If there is no money due

EXAMPLE 17

Valuation

Quantity Surveyor

Works

Valuation No:
Date of issue
QS Reference

To Architect/S.O.

I/We have made, under the terms of the Contract, an Interim Valuation

as at   † and I/we report as follows:–

Gross Valuation
(excluding any work or material notified to me/us by the Architect/S.O. in writing, as not being in accordance with the Contract).   £

Less Total Amount of Retention, as attached Statement.   £

Less total amount stated as due in Interim Certificates previously issued by the Architect/S.O. up to and including Interim Certificate No . . . .   £

£

Balance (in words)   £

Employer

Signature: Quantity Surveyor

Contractor

Notes:
(i)   All the above amounts are exclusive of V.A.T.
(ii)   The balance stated is subject to any statutory deductions which the Employer may be obliged to make under the provisions of the Finance (No. 2) Act 1975 where the Employer is classed as a "contractor" for the purposes of the Act.
(iii)   It is assumed that the Architect/S.O. will:–
        (a) satisfy himself that there is no further work or material which is not in accordance with the Contract
        (b) notify Nominated Sub-contractors of payments directed for them and of Retention held by the Employer.
        (c) satisfy himself that previous payments directed for Nominated Sub-contractors have been discharged.
† (iv) The Architect/S.O.'s Interim Certificate should be issued within seven days of the date indicated thus
(v)   Action by the Contractor should be taken on the basis of figures in, or attached to, the Architect/S.O.'s Interim Certificate.

Contract sum   £

© 1980 RICS

108

EXAMPLE 18

Statement of Retention and of Nominated Sub-Contractors Values

Quantity Surveyor   Works

This Statement relates to :-
Valuation No:
Date of issue
OS Reference

| | Gross Valuation | Amount subject to: | | | Amount of Retention | Net Valuation | Amount Previously Certified | Balance |
		Full Retention of %	Half Retention of %	No Retention				
	£	£	£	£	£	£	£	£
Main Contractor								
Nominated Sub-Contractors:-								
TOTAL								

No account has been taken of any discounts for cash to which the Contractor may be entitled if discharging the balance within 17 days of the issue of the Architect/S.O.'s Certificate.
The sums stated are exclusive of V.A.T.

© 1980 RICS

109

to the contractor under the next interim certificate then the direct payment to the sub-contractor must be made within the 14-day period within which the contractor would have been paid.

There is no obligation on the employer to make direct payments to nominated sub-contractors in excess of the amount due to the contractor. If the amount due to the contractor is retention which is being released then the amount by which the payment to the contractor is reduced in respect of a direct payment must not exceed the contractor's share of the released retention.

If there is more than one nominated sub-contractor to be paid direct and the monies due to the contractor are insufficient to meet the total of the direct payments then the employer must apportion the money available pro rata or on some other fair and reasonable basis.

If the contractor goes into liquidation these provisions for direct payment to nominated sub-contractors immediately cease to have effect.

Valuation and certificate forms

The changes in the rules regarding retention have necessitated the revision of the standard forms used by the professional advisers in the administration of contracts.

The valuation form published by the RICS for the use of the quantity surveyor is shown in example 17 and the Statement of Retention and of Nominated Sub-Contractor's Values, which accompanies the valuation form as an appendix, is shown in example 18. These forms are published in separate pads and each pad contains notes on their application.

It will be seen that there are several notes on the valuation form itself which are a useful reminder of the contractual obligations. It will also be seen that the form requires two dates to be inserted: the date of issue by the quantity surveyor and, in the text of the valuation, the date on which the valuation was actually prepared.

The appendix brings on to one form the details of amounts included for nominated sub-contractors, upon which the architect has to issue his directions to the contractor, and the statement of retention which must be issued in accordance with the new rules.

New forms for the architect's interim certificate and the direction of amounts due to nominated sub-contractors, together with the statement of retention, are being published by the RIBA and will be available by the time the 1980 Standard Form is in use.

7: COMPLETION AND THE FINAL ACCOUNT

(See also Chapter 7: pages 58–65)

Provisions regarding completion of the works are virtually unchanged in the 1980 Standard Form and although the certificate of practical completion is no longer required as authority for releasing part of the retention, it is still required in connection with the other aspects of the contract which are dependent upon it, namely the commencement of the defects liability period, the ending of the contractor's insurance obligations, the commencement of the period of final measurement and the opening of arbitration proceedings in respect of those matters which cannot be dealt with in arbitration until after practical completion.

Final account

The responsibilities of the contractor and the quantity surveyor in connection with the final account are set out at the beginning of clause 30.6. These may be summarized as follows:

— Either before or within a reasonable time after practical completion the contractor shall send to the architect or quantity surveyor all the documents necessary for preparing the final account.
— Subject to the contractor complying with that obligation, the quantity surveyor will prepare the final account or, as it is described in the conditions, 'a statement of all the final valuations under clause 13 including those relating to the work of the nominated sub-contractors'. That statement must be prepared within the period of final measurement and valuation as stated in the appendix.
— When the final account has been completed the architect must send a copy of the statement of the final valuations to the contractor and the relevant extract therefrom to each nominated sub-contractor.

Clause 30.6 goes on to set out in tabulated form all those matters which must be dealt with in the final account in order to adjust the contract sum in accordance with the conditions. These may be summarized as follows:

To be deducted
1. Prime cost sums and amounts in respect of named sub-contractors, together with contractor's profit.
2. Provisional sums and work described as provisional.
3. Variations which are omissions including, where appropriate, omissions in respect of other works carried out under changed conditions as a result of variations.
4. Amounts allowable to the employer under the fluctuations clauses.
5. Any other amount which is required by the contract to be deducted from the contract sum.

To be added

6. The total amounts of nominated sub-contracts finally adjusted in accordance with the relevant sub-contract conditions.
7. Where the contractor has tendered for work which was to have been carried out by a nominated sub-contractor and his tender has been accepted, the amount of that tender adjusted in accordance with the terms of the tender.
8. The final amounts due to nominated suppliers, including cash discounts of 5%, but excluding value added tax.
9. The contractor's profit on 6,7 and 8 above.
10. Any amounts payable by the employer in respect of statutory fees and charges, setting out the works, opening up and testing, royalties, remedial works where the architect authorizes payment and insurances under clause 20.2.3 (formerly 19(2)(a)).
11. Additions in respect of variations including, where appropriate, additions in respect of other works carried out under changed conditions as a result of variations.
12. The value of work carried out against provisional sums or provisional quantities included in the contract bills.
13. Any amounts payable by the employer to the contractor by way of reimbursement for loss and expense arising from matters materially affecting the regular progress of the works or from the discovery of antiquities.
14. Any amount expended by the contractor as a result of loss or damage by fire or other perils where those risks are insured by the employer and the contractor is entitled to recover such amounts.
15. Any amount payable to the contractor under the fluctuations clauses.
16. Any other amount which is required by the contract to be added to the contract sum.

Final certificate

The final certificate must be issued by the architect within 3 months of the end of the defects liability period or of the completion of making good defects or of the receipt by the architect or the quantity surveyor of the documents necessary to compile the final account, whichever is the latest date.

The amount of the final certificate is the amount of difference between the total of the final account and the amounts previously stated as due under interim certificates. This shows a difference of wording from the 1963 Standard Form in which the final certificate was the difference between the total of the final account and the amount previously paid to the contractor. The clause as now worded preserves the contractor's rights to any money previously certified which the employer may not have paid.

The new provision referred to in section 6 which requires the architect to issue an interim certificate which includes the final amounts due to all nominated sub-contractors not less than 28 days before the issue of the final certificate means that the final certificate itself would not include any further payments in respect of nominated sub-contractors. However, the architect must notify all nominated sub-contractors of the date of issue of the final certificate.

8: DELAYS AND DISPUTES

(See also Chapter 8: pages 66–71)

Of the definitions referred to in the introduction to this addendum two have particular significance in relation to the works being delayed. These are:

— 'Completion Date', which is defined as 'the Date for Completion as fixed and stated in the Appendix or any date fixed under either clause 25 (extension of time) or clause 33.1.3 (effect of war damage)'.

— 'Relevant Event', which is described as 'any one of the events set out in clause 25.4', which deals with the circumstances which may entitle the contractor to an extension of time.

The relevant events referred to above include all those matters previously set out in clause 23 of the 1963 Standard Form with some significant amendments and additions. The amendments are:

— 'Exceptionally inclement weather' has been changed to 'Exceptionally adverse weather conditions'. This change has been made so that exceptionally hot weather, which can hardly be described as inclement but which may well delay construction works, is now covered by the provision.

— The old clause 23(j), delay due to the contractor's inability for reasons beyond his control to obtain the necessary labour or materials, is no longer an optional clause.

The additional causes of delay now included as relevant events are:

— Delay in the supply by the employer of materials or goods which the employer has agreed to provide for the works or his failure to supply those materials and goods.

— Delay due to action by the Government which restricts the availability or supply of labour or materials.

— Delay due to failure of the employer to give in due time access to or from the site in accordance with the contract documents.

Procedure in the event of delay

In the event of one of the relevant events occurring, the procedure leading to extension of time is set out in clause 25 and may be summarized as follows:

— Immediately it becomes reasonably apparent that the progress of the works is being delayed or is likely to be delayed the contractor must give written notice to the architect of the material circumstances stating the cause of the delay and identifying the relevant event.

— If the circumstances referred to above include reference to a nominated sub-contractor a copy of the written notice must be sent to the sub-contractor concerned.

— In respect of each and every relevant event the contractor must in the notice or as soon as possible give in writing particulars of the expected effects of the relevant event and an estimate of the extent of the expected delay.

— Again where a nominated sub-contractor is involved, copies of the particulars and the estimate of the delay must be sent to the sub-contractor concerned.

— After the necessary notice has been given in the first place the contractor must keep the architect up to date with all matters arising from the relevant event, including any material changes in the particulars of the expected effects or the estimate of the extent of the delay.

— After he has received the notice of possible delay together with the particulars of the expected effects of the relevant event and the estimate of the extent of the delay, the architect must decide whether the works are likely to be delayed beyond the completion date and whether that delay is due to the relevant event referred to .

— If the architect is satisfied that there will be a delay and the relevant event has caused it he must in writing give an extension of time by fixing such later completion date as he estimates to be fair and reasonable.

— When fixing the later completion date the architect must state, also in writing, which of the relevant events he has taken into account and the extent, if any, to which he has had regard to any variations involving the omission of the work which may have been issued since the previous completion date had been fixed.

The architect must fix the new completion date not later than 12 weeks from the receipt of the written notice of delay from the contractor or from the subsequent receipt of sufficient particulars and estimate of the extent of the delay. If the period between the receipt of the notice and the necessary particulars and the previously

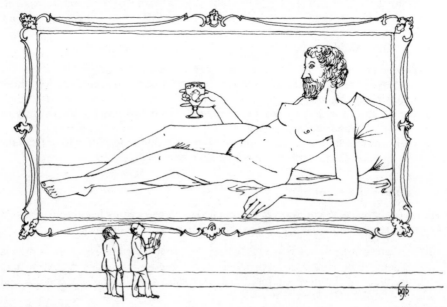

Relevant event:
"Well, the story is that the sittings went on so long the model turned out to be trans-sexual and became a man before the picture was done"

fixed completion date is less than 12 weeks then the architect must fix a revised completion date before the previously fixed completion date is reached.

Once the architect has granted an extension of time and fixed a later completion date he may subsequently amend that date to an earlier date if, after granting his extension of time, he has subsequently issued an instruction requiring as a variation the omission of any of the work, provided he is satisfied that it is fair and reasonable to do so. He cannot, however, fix a completion date which is earlier than the original completion date stated in the appendix to the conditions of contract.

Not later than 12 weeks after the date of practical completion the architect must finalize the position regarding the completion date by taking one of three courses of action, namely:

— By fixing a completion date later than that previously fixed if in his opinion it is fair and reasonable to do so having regard to any of the relevant events, whether upon reviewing a previous decision or otherwise, and whether or not the relevant event has been specifically notified to him.
— By fixing a completion date earlier than that previously fixed if in his opinion it is fair and reasonable to do so having regard to any instruction requiring as a variation the omission of any work which he may have issued after the last occasion on which he made an extension of time.
— By confirming to the contractor the completion date previously fixed.

Whichever of these courses of action the architect takes he must put the matter in writing to the contractor.

All the conditions regarding the granting of extensions of time are subject to the proviso that the contractor shall constantly use his best endeavours to prevent delay in the progress of the works, howsoever caused, and prevent the completion of the works being delayed or further delayed beyond the completion date; and also that he shall do all that may be reasonably required to the satisfaction of the architect to proceed with the works.

Finally it should be noted that whenever the architect fixes a new completion date he must notify every nominated sub-contractor of his decision.

There is little doubt that the 1980 Standard Form imposes upon both the contractor and the architect clear and not inconsiderable obligations whenever there is a likelihood of delay. When seeking an extension of time the contractor must be much more specific than has been the case in the past and the architect must deal with the matter when it arises. The intention of the contract is quite clear. Decisions on extensions of time are to be made as quickly as possible after the relevant event which is likely to cause delay has occurred. The common practice of waiting to see what the delay actually is at the end of the contract and then arguing about whether or not an extension of time is justified has no place under the new conditions.

It must be remembered that in the normal course of events the architect will be assisted by the new contractual obligations on the contractor to provide and keep up to date a master programme for the execution of the works. Perhaps the greatest difficulty which will be encountered in the new procedure will be in deciding whether or not the notice, particulars and estimates which the contractor is required to provide are sufficient for the architect to make his decision on extending the completion date. This will require close co-operation between contractor and architect and it is to be hoped that architects will be decisive in the matter and will not use alleged insufficiency of particulars and estimates as an excuse for delaying the issue of extensions of time.

Liquidated damages

If the contractor fails to complete the works by the completion date the architect must issue a certificate to that effect and the employer may then exercise his right to receive damages for non-completion from the contractor. The provisions regarding damages have not materially changed from previous editions of the contract but the architect's certificate will now be linked to the review of the extension of time which he is required to carry out during the 12 weeks after practical completion.

Whether or not the contractor is required to pay liquidated damages is now entirely at the discretion of the employer, but if he does intend to claim liquidated damages he must give notice of his intention to do so before the architect issues the final certificate.

Reimbursement of loss and/or expense

Several of the relevant events referred to earlier in this section, the occurrence of which may entitle the contractor to an extension of time, may also entitle him to be reimbursed for any direct loss and/or expense which he may incur as a result of the relevant event concerned materially affecting the regular progress of the works. The relevant events concerned are those which may be regarded as being under the control of the employer or the architect. These are listed in clause 26.2 and may be summarized as follows:

— Failure of the architect to provide the contractor at the proper time with the necessary instructions, drawings, details or levels.
— The opening up of work for inspection or testing, which is subsequently found to be in accordance with the contract.
— Discrepancies between the contract documents.
— The execution of work by the employer or by others not forming part of the contract, or the failure to execute such work.
— The supply by the employer of materials and goods which he has agreed to supply, or his failure to supply.
— Architect's instructions regarding postponement of work.
— Failure of the employer to give in due time access to or from the site in accordance with the contract documents.
— Architect's instruction requiring a variation or in regard to the expenditure of provisional sums.

If the contractor considers he has incurred, or is likely to incur, direct loss and/or expense as a result of one of the matters listed he must make a written application to the architect. This application must be made as soon as it becomes apparent that the regular progress of the works is being, or will be, affected. The contractor must give the architect as much information as he can and, when required to do so, he must submit to the architect or to the quantity surveyor such details as they may reasonably require to ascertain the loss and/or expense.

As soon as it is possible to do so the architect or, if he so instructs, the quantity surveyor, must ascertain the amount of loss and/or expense and the amount so ascertained must be included in the next interim certificate.

It must be borne in mind that the fact that the contractor may be granted an extension of time as a result of one of the relevant events listed above does not necessarily mean that he is automatically entitled to some financial reimbursement.

He must show that the relevant event has caused him loss and/or expense which he will not recover under any other provision in the contract.

Conversely it should be borne in mind that the occurrence of one of the relevant events listed above may not justify an extension of time, but the contractor may still be entitled to reimbursement of loss and/or expense which he incurs as a result of that event.

Disputes and arbitration

In the event of a dispute occurring which cannot be settled by agreement between the parties then the matter must be referred to arbitration. The only exceptions to this provision are disputes in relation to the statutory tax deduction scheme insofar as legislation provides other methods of settling such disputes; disputes arising from the employer's right under the VAT agreement to challenge the amount of tax claimed by the contractor; and, in the case of the Local Authorities edition, disputes under the fair wages clause.

As indicated earlier the agreement to refer disputes to arbitration is now incorporated in the articles of agreement and is set out in detail in article 5.

The main change from the arbitration clause in previous editions of the contract is the introduction of 'joinder' provisions under which separate but related disputes may be dealt with together before the same arbitrator. Thus, where there is a dispute between the employer and the contractor on the one hand, and a dispute on related issues between the contractor and a nominated sub-contractor or nominated supplier on the other hand, and where the arbitrator is a suitably qualified person to hear both disputes, the arbitrator may direct that the two references may be joined together in the arbitration proceedings.

The arbitration provisions still limit the matters which can be dealt with prior to practical completion, but the scope of this proviso has been widened and the matters which may now be brought before the arbitrator while the works are still in progress are as follows:

1. Dispute arising in connection with the appointment of a new architect or quantity surveyor in accordance with the articles of agreement.
2. Dispute as to whether an architect's instruction is valid.
3. Dispute as to whether a certificate has been improperly withheld or has not been properly prepared in accordance with the contract conditions.
4. Dispute arising in connection with the employment by the employer of others to carry out work when the contractor has failed to comply with an architect's instruction.
5. Dispute in connection with an application for an extension of time.
6. Dispute arising in connection with an outbreak of hostilities or with war damage.

INDEX

Numbers in bold type refer to Supplement

INDEX

119

INDEX